I DON'T WANT TO, I DON'T FEEL LIKE IT

HOW RESISTANCE CONTROLS YOUR LIFE AND WHAT TO DO ABOUT IT

Published by Keep It Simple Books
Printed in the United States of America

Cover design by Marie Denkinger
sunwheelart@earthlink.net
Cover art by Alex Mill

Illustrations by
June Shiver
Ashwini Narayanan
Cheri Huber

TABLE OF CONTENTS

Preface

DEFINING RESISTANCE 1

Defining Resistance 5

Resistance: An Ego-identity Maintenance System 7

Exiting the Ego-Identity Maintenance System 17

THE HOW OF RESISTANCE 19

STUDENT and SAGE #1 20

The Importance of How 21

STUDENT and SAGE #2 23

Distraction 24

STUDENT and SAGE #3 29

To Get Past Resistance, We Have to Get Past Feeling Bad. 29

STUDENT and SAGE #4 37

Resistance: A point of view 38

"Knowing" as Resistance 40

STUDENT and SAGE #5 49

Resistance: The Voice of the Internal Authority 50

STUDENT and SAGE #6 54

The Big Fat Illusion 55

The Negativity of I 61

STUDENT and SAGE #7 68

A Life-Stealing Story 69

There's Nothing Wrong, and... 72

Attending to the Life We Want 74

STUDENT and SAGE #8 76

Losing Interest in How "I" Feels 78

STUDENT and SAGE #9 85

No Change in Consciousness without a Change in Behavior 86

The Difference between Behavior and Being 88

Resistance as Resistance 90

FORMS OF RESISTANCE 93

It's Hard to Be Present. 94
Resistance to Repetition 97
Hope as Resistance 99
Resistance to Committing 101
Overwhelm as Resistance 102
"I Don't Want To, You Can't Make Me" as Resistance 105
Fear as Resistance 107
Anxiety as Resistance 109
"Do I Deserve It?" as Resistance 111
Resistance to Impermanence 113
Resistance to Guidance 118
Comparison as Resistance 121
Liking and Disliking as Resistance 123
Agonizing Over Decisions as Resistance 125
If I Am, I Cannot Do: Resistance to Being 127
Resistance as "Not Enough Time" 130
Resistance to Practicing When Things Are Going Well 133
Resistance and the Illusion of Control 135

AWARENESS: The Antidote to Resistance 141

A Student/Sage Interaction 142
A Change of Direction 152

TOOLS FOR GARDEN LIVING: A 30-Day Retreat 153

Fifteen 2-Day Exercises 154-194
Bonus Round 195-202

A REVIEW OF WHERE WE ARE 203

Recipe for Awareness 207
An Invitation from Life 207

THIS BOOK IN "OTHER WORDS" 211

A collection of quotes 211

Dharma is the teaching, the understanding, the contents of the enlightened mind. It is the experience of the joy of intelligence knowing itself.

-- from The Daily Recollection, recited at the Zen Monastery Peace Center

A LITERARY SPIRITUAL JOURNEY

THE KEY

GUIDE TO ENDING SUFFERING THROUGH AWARENESS AND THE NAME OF THE KEY IS PRACTICE WILLINGNESS

BE THE PERSON YOU WANT TO FIND

THE DEPRESSION BOOK

THE FEAR BOOK

OVERCOMING OBSTACLES

SELF-HATE AND JUDGMENT AS OBSTACLES TO COMPASSIONATE SELF-ACCEPTANCE

REGARDLESS OF WHAT YOU WERE TAUGHT TO BELIEVE... THERE IS NOTHING WRONG WITH YOU

REASSURING THE LITTLE CHILD

WHAT YOU PRACTICE IS WHAT YOU HAVE

FINDING THE COMPASSIONATE MENTOR AND EMBRACING THE SUFFERING HUMAN

RECORDING & LISTENING

ROAD BLOCK OF RESISTANCE

I DON'T WANT TO, I DON'T FEEL LIKE IT

IDENTIFYING AND DROPPING THE RESISTANCE OF EGO IDENTITY

Preface

In 1984, we published *The Key and the Name of the Key Is Willingness* because we thought it contained just about everything necessary to guide a person to wake up and end suffering through practicing awareness. The book was transformative for many, but it soon became obvious that it was not the miracle we'd hoped for. People were suffering as mightily as ever. Something was missing.

In subsequent books we addressed specific content, such as fear, depression, and relationship to illustrate the principles of Awareness Practice--very helpful in many ways, but not quite the revolution we envisioned.

What eventually came to light was that people won't end suffering because they feel unworthy, and we realized that sense of unworthiness is a product of self-hate. The recognition and exploration of the process of self-hate inspired *There Is Nothing Wrong with You* (1993).

People were now able to recognize the **conversation** in their heads that was causing distress. Gaining some distance from the conversation brought the realization that there's an active **process** that causes us to feel bad.

We don't feel bad because we **are** bad, we feel bad because we're listening to a self-hating conversation telling us we're bad...

Am I a loser?

Duh! yes, you are a loser.

SUFFERING HUMAN

INTERNAL VOICE OF AUTHORITY

The work of *There Is Nothing Wrong with You* allowed us to step back from and observe the **process** of suffering. From that vantage point we could see **how** suffering works and stop taking it personally. We could stop believing the voices were there because there was something wrong with us. In mentoring the young parts of ourselves, we could open to the possibility of embracing all aspects of ourselves in unconditional love and acceptance.

A part of the work of going beyond self-hate is making recordings of "reassurances," accurate information about ourselves in direct opposition to the self-hating voices.

And yet, even able to see all of that, people continued to listen to and believe the judgmental, punishing, cruel voices.

Even worse, their suffering now included "Why are you still suffering? You should know better!"

The net result of this work seemed to lead to focusing on the **process of suffering** rather than practicing the **process of ending suffering**. In other words, people began to focus on their relationship with the voices of self-hate instead of turning attention to unconditional love.

Several years later, reassurances grew into the Recording and Listening practice presented in *What You Practice is What You Have* (2010). This tool is completely revolutionizing our Awareness Practice. Recording and Listening provides a replicative way to experience the compassionate wisdom of our authentic nature. The ability to access authenticity enables us to develop a practice of choosing wisdom and compassion instead of the messages of self-hate and suffering.

Suddenly, we had a tangible, reliable way to practice having--and being--what our hearts have always wanted.

Traditionally, spiritual seekers go to spiritual teachers to have wisdom imparted. The teacher is the holder of the wisdom; the sincere student is the recipient of the wisdom. This tradition has perpetuated the notion that wisdom comes from outside of us and is in the possession of a select few. The belief is that if we work hard and are "good students," some of what we receive might stick. But it is unlikely that we would ever become repositories of wisdom.

Wonderfully, with Recording and Listening
people began to have an undeniable experience
of the same wisdom they had
seen and recognized outside
appearing inside.

It's not that "we" hold that wisdom. It's that the wisdom we've been seeking is as accessible directly as it has been via an external authority.*

People began to recognize intuition and insight, realizing that "knowing" is something that "drops in," with or without an external mirror in the form of a

* We're not supportive of the notion often bandied about that "everything I'm seeking is inside me." We're describing a very different process. The wisdom, love, and compassion that is the authentic nature of a human being does not reside within the "I" of ego. It is not housed in a "me" or a "we." We go beyond the ego sense of "I" and drop the sense of a "me" when we touch true nature. (In this same way we don't talk about "loving myself." Compassion for the "self" is very different from an egocentric relationship in which an "I" is "loving" itself.)

teacher. (We are not saying that a teacher is unnecessary. If we don't have a wise and trusted guide, we will surely be guided by ego.) It became obvious that accessing wisdom, love, and compassion is possible only when the attention is not on the self-hating voices in the head.

Recording and Listening
practice has proved to us beyond doubt
that "the quality of our lives is determined by the
focus of our attention."

Focusing attention on

love,

kindness,

generosity,

compassion,

spaciousness,

and gratitude

results in direct experience
of the joy of presence in life.

And yet,
even having
direct experience
that what we seek is
immediately available,
knowing from personal
experience that there's
a method to access it,

people still slid back
into the familiar grooves
of listening to
and believing
the self-hating
conversation in the head.

And then one day it dawned:

RESISTANCE

is the culprit!

This book explores
the process of resistance
to having the life we want.

We do not attempt
an exhaustive exploration of
either Awareness Practice or resistance.

We simply show common ways
resistance sabotages us,
leading to failure and unhappiness, and

we present tried-and-true practices
for developing a more authentic orientation
to life.

EG For fun, we created this symbol for "ego-I" and sprinkled it throughout the illustrations. It represents the system that creates and maintains the illusion of a separate self, which we refer to as:

egocentric karmic conditioning/self-hate
conditioned mind
ego-identity
conditioning
identity
ego-I
ego

Gasshō,
Cheri and Ashwini

P.S. This book is not meant to be read in the conventional sense of the word. It is not meant to be intellectually understood, but intuitively savored. It is based in Awareness Practice. Sit with it, stop often, sense what it says, and do the exercises. Notice what arises as you read it. Open to it perhaps with the attitude of mind that Rumi suggests in this verse:

Sell your cleverness and buy bewilderment;
Cleverness is mere opinion, bewilderment is intuition.

DEFINING RESISTANCE

I don't want to,
I don't feel like it.

There's an impulse:
-- I want to lose weight, eat better, join the gym.
-- I want to meditate. I'm going to go to bed early, get more sleep so I can get up early and sit.
-- I want to do something that lights me up.
-- I'm going to stop wasting time, stop watching tv, limit my time on the computer, stop playing those games!

There's excitement, enthusiasm, and anticipation. We can see our new life, the way we'll be when we're doing all the things we want to do the way we want to do them.

Yes!

And right on the heels of excited enthusiasm is a subtle, or not so subtle, voice-in-the-head campaign that starts to leach out the elation and excitement.

The messages go something like this:

won't stick
with it...

might as well
quit now...

too tired...

always
fail...

too hard...

don't feel
like it...

wait until
tomorrow...

Before long we find ourselves still not meditating, not eating well, not getting enough rest, definitely not lit up, and what "I want to do" isn't happening-- again!

Then, at some point, we feel the inevitable, "What's wrong with me? Why can't I make my life work?"

And, all the feeling bad in the world doesn't change a thing.

If you recognize this trap/bamboozle/loop (perhaps as a result of years of failed self-improvement plans), you've most likely spent a lot of time and energy trying to figure out why this is happening. "Why do I keep failing?" And, you've probably heard plenty of internal "advice" about what you should do differently, usually amounting to "just try harder."

Since this book is based in Awareness Practice, we're going to take a different approach. And when we do, we notice a few things we may not have considered before.

1. There is a desire for something to be different from "what is."
2. There is a "someone" who has to be different.
3. What that "someone" wants has never come to pass.
4. There is a tremendous amount of suffering as a consequence.

In other words, each time we embark on doing something we "want to do," we end up frustrated and dissatisfied.

Defining Resistance

The Buddha taught that life is "dukkha" or suffering. Perhaps a better translation for dukkha is dissatisfaction. Even in the best of times, most human beings live with an undercurrent of dissatisfaction, wanting something to be different, improved, or modified, resulting in a "better life."

A good definition of dissatisfaction might be "wanting something other than what is," or "resisting what is."

Human beings have the ability to imagine a reality other than what is. This creates the illusion* of a "someone" that appears to be outside of and separate from what is.

In this book, we call this illusion of separation "I," "ego-identity," or "ego-I."

Moment by moment, "I" creates its imaginary world by assessing and evaluating what is, comparing it to what it should be and judging it for what it's not. This process keeps alive the imaginary world of "what's not," "what's wrong," and "what's missing."

* It's an illusion because it's imaginary, not true, not real.

Ego-I rejects what IS.
It is the process of dissatisfaction.

Said another way...

-- Ego-I clings firmly to a point of view that life can (and should) be other than what is.
-- Its perspective is that there is something wrong with what is.
-- It operates on the premise that it can change what it is dissatisfied with and that those changes will lead to a different, and better, outcome.

Because ego-I is not real, its illusory world must constantly be maintained. Its maintenance strategy is resisting anything that suggests that it is not real. It opposes anything that threatens its imaginary point of view or its illusory existence.

Resistance--
I don't want to,
I don't feel like it,
I can't, I won't--
is the process
by which "I" maintains itself.

Resistance: An Ego-identity Maintenance System

Each of us is born a jewel, a unique expression of the Intelligence that animates.

Before long we encounter the social context we are born into and begin adapting to survive that environment. As we move through the stages of socialization, layers of conditioning form around us, like a crust.

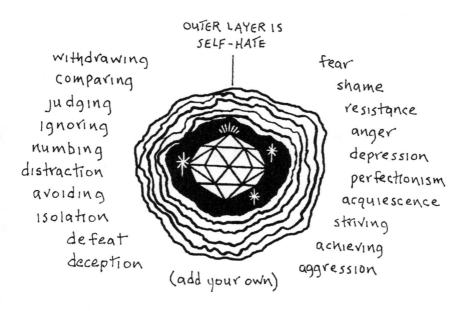

OUTER LAYER IS
SELF-HATE

withdrawing
comparing
judging
ignoring
numbing
distraction
avoiding
isolation
defeat
deception

fear
shame
resistance
anger
depression
perfectionism
acquiescence
striving
achieving
aggression

(add your own)

Slowly we are distanced from our authentic being, unconsciously developing an elaborate survival system, a rock sheath (to continue our mineralogical metaphor) that solidifies into an identity, a belief system of "who I am" that defines our orientation to life.

As we identify more and more with the crust, we forget the experience of ourselves as the jewel.

Social conditioning teaches us that we must do whatever is necessary to survive. We must follow the program exactly or we are bad and wrong and must be punished. We learn to fear and hate 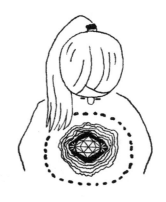 ourselves when we aren't the way we're supposed to be and don't do what we're supposed to do.

We recognize this system when we tune in to the constant loop of voices in our heads talking us into believing their programmed "reality." We call these the voices of self-hate (they are hateful!) and this survival system, this crusty layer:

egocentric karmic conditioning.

Egocentric -- the illusion of being a separate self, the ego-identity, the "I" at the center of the universe that claims things should be different from what they are

Karmic -- the sum total of everything it has taken to produce you since before the beginning of beginningless time

Conditioning -- Our adaptation to the life circumstances we were born into; the process that creates and maintains the identity that plays out its karma in the social context it is born into.

Self-hate keeps the survival system in place through cruel, judgmental messages, reinforcing the belief that "everything that's wrong in your life is your fault." The human being could be living life as an exquisite jewel but, instead, believes himself/herself to be the survival system rock sheath of fear, anxiety, depression, conflict, negativity, and struggle.

The function of a survival system is to guarantee its survival at all costs, and it resists anything that threatens it.

Resistance is the reaction of the crust, the ego-identity, the survival system, to the possibility of living from the jewel.

Crust: I feel pressured and anxious.

Jewel: I want to meditate. Meditation is the experience of peace.

Crust: But I'm pressured and anxious. I'd like to meditate too, but there's so much to do, so little time. I don't want to right now. I'll do it later. (Later never comes.)

The ego-identity survival system
we're up against
has some really impressive
defense strategies!

HERE ARE SOME OF THEM:

-- **Incorporating the human in its defense**
The most pernicious outcome of social conditioning is that we believe the identity that has been created-- this "self," this aggregation of beliefs and assumptions--is what we really are.

The survival system's strategy to maintain itself is to make us believe that we are what the resistance is protecting--the illusion of a separate self. This leaves us asking, "Why would I want to dismantle a system that's protecting me? I'm not a fool!"

We identify with the crust so completely that we feel threatened by anything that would free us.

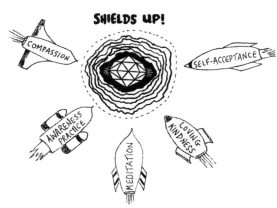

We experience any attempts to return to the jewel as a threat to survival. We feel the crust's resistance as **our** resistance and spend all our energy and resources defending the survival system.

-- Controlling the point of view

The crust is the default lens through which we view the world. It is a very limited perspective. Through that contracted viewpoint everything is limited: what we are, what the world is, what everyone else is. As long as we are identified with the crust, it's impossible to see anything beyond its limitations.

The world looks pretty rocky to me...

It is not possible to experience ourselves as the jewel through the lens of the crust.

The survival system controls what we see and how we see it, ensuring we will never be open to anything that contradicts the system. It's a thorough brainwashing. It is what we're used to, it's "the water we swim in," and because it "feels" so true and accurate, we almost never question its veracity. In fact, it's what we consult to reinforce our identity and confirm the accuracy of our perceptions. As long as

Should I be worried?

Yes, you should be worried!

oh... ok...

we are within ego-identity, we cannot get beyond it because built into it is the resistance to seeing it.

Crust: What a mess I made of that meeting. I hate it when I get put on the spot. I can never think of anything to say.

Colleague: That's not true. It went quite well I thought.

Crust: You're just saying that to make me feel better.

We're brainwashed to believe
we aren't brainwashed
so that we will resist every suggestion
that we are brainwashed.
We will violently oppose
contrary information from "outside,"
fearing an attempt to brainwash us!
All this brainwashing serves to
guarantee that the survival system
maintains control over our experience.

-- **Putting ego in charge of figuring it out**
Because we see "ourselves" and the "world" through
the lens of the crust, we cannot see the resistance
of the survival system as the process of ego-identity
maintenance that it is.

When faced with a problem such as "I want to but I
can't," our default orientation is to engage the
survival system in solving the problem. "I" is
assigned the task of "figuring it out." An old
expression that captures this scenario perfectly is,
"Putting the fox in charge of the henhouse."

Putting the ego
in charge of
transcending the ego
guarantees the ego
will survive.

We cannot see that attempting to let go of dissatisfaction (I want it to be different) through the same process that's been holding it in place (I want it to be different) is the way to keep it in place, not the way to let it go.

We repeatedly use this approach of figuring it out and trying harder, each time running into a

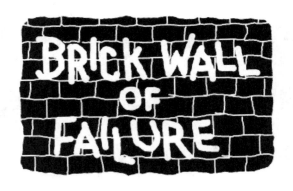

If the same approach,
used repeatedly,
results in the same outcome,
then it's time to realize that
it's the approach that's the problem,
not the outcome,
and not the person making the effort.

Exiting the Ego-Identity Maintenance System

So where does that leave us with our problem of "I don't want to. I don't feel like it"? Faced with a problem, almost everyone wants to start with the why questions.

"Why don't I want to?"
"Why don't I feel like it?"
"Why is it like this?"
"Why do we have resistance?"

Or the very dangerous question posed by resistance itself, "If we have resistance, it must be serving some good purpose, right?"

Instead of focusing on the why, we are going to focus on the HOW. HOW does resistance operate and HOW does it accomplish what it accomplishes? Putting our attention on this question allows us to learn some very interesting things.

Up next: a journey through the how of resistance.

THE HOW
OF RESISTANCE

STUDENT and SAGE # 1

Student: I want to meditate. I've tried many times and I always quit. I really want to do it but I can't seem to make myself stick with it. This seems to be true of a lot of things that I want to do for myself, things that take care of me.

Sage: How?

Student: How? I'm not sure I know what you mean.

Sage: How are you not able to meditate? You must find out how you are not able to meditate if you are ever to be able to meditate. The way to do that is to go home and meditate, watching closely how "not able to meditate" happens. Then come back and tell me your experience of how you're not able to meditate.

The Importance of How

When we ask "how," we open ourselves to observation, to noticing, to being present with what is actually happening. There is a fresh, curious, attitude of inquiry, a willingness to gather information without judgment or evaluation.

> Asking "how" moves us into
> awareness of what is,
> instead of seeing the world
> as a problem to be solved.

"How" serves another important function. "How" allows us to get a sense of Life as a "process"-- dynamic, active, lively, changing, moving, mutable, unfolding. Nothing in Life is static. But we are conditioned to define, limit, abstract and assign labels to everything we encounter as a way to wrap our heads around it, make sense of it, understand it and interact with it. This may appear to be a convenient way to be in the world, but we lose Life's vibrancy and aliveness when we put things in tidy boxes.

As the old Zen saying goes, you cannot experience a river by capturing a bucketful and examining it.

When we live in how, we open ourselves to being informed by the Intelligence animating all. The barriers erected by what and why ("What am I doing wrong, and why can't I fix it?") fall away, and we enter the dynamic process that is Life living. In that movement, questions and answers fall away in an experience of what is.

Developing the skill of looking at the how of things gives us a new lens, a new way to explore the process of resistance, of "I don't want to, I don't feel like it."

We stop asking "What's wrong?" and start asking "How does this work?"

STUDENT and SAGE #2

Student: Here's what I saw. I planned to meditate. I tried to meditate. But I never actually ended up meditating. There was always something else I had to do instead. There was no

time for it, or if there was time it was not the right time. I got interrupted, I overslept, I forgot, I was tired. Maybe it's just not something I can do. And the one time I did get on the cushion, I just fidgeted and all I could hear in my head was "I hate this, this is boring." I got anxious and gave up.

> Time to meditate...
> One... two... three
> ...four... five...

> ...really need to do laundry ...nothing clean to wear...

> ...she'll be here in an hour ...the kitchen's a mess...

> ...need to text him and ask why he did that...

> ...sixteen...seventeen... eighteen...... AAARG! I'm no good at this!

> ...should get up and do something useful...

Sage: Can you see you are caught in a process of not meditating instead of engaged with a process of meditating?

Student: Yes. I can see that. What should I do?

Sage: Look to see what you get as a result of remaining the person who can't. There is a payoff for everything we do and don't do. What is the payoff for continuing to be a person who can't?

Distraction

As we see how not meditating happens, we become aware of a constant conversation that distracts us from keeping the attention on what's here and now.

Many of us know the experience of sitting down on the cushion and becoming aware of a voice in the head talking about a list of urgent to-dos. The laundry, the

dishes, that email I have to send, an inspiration for the presentation I've been working on, the text from a friend that just came in--a to-do list that is so critically important it must be attended to right now but didn't show up until the moment I decided to meditate!

Other familiar voices:

-- the self-doubting you-can't-do-it-and-should-quit voice

-- the fantasy voice that seduces me into visions of myself in a perfect place meditating in complete bliss

-- the critical voice that complains that I'm not doing it right and has endless advice about how to do it differently, e.g., my body shouldn't hurt, I should pay better attention, I should modify the meditation instructions so it's easier for me, I should follow the instructions exactly

-- the "helpful" voice that gives me a list of all that I could do to support my meditation practice: buy a new cushion, soundproof the living room, get fresh flowers, sign up for a meditation class

-- the voice of procrastination that suggests that later would be a better time to meditate because I really am too hungry or too tired just now

-- and the voice with the most "important" advice of all: I shouldn't be distracted!

The conversation starts up and the outcome is the same: a distracted, resistant human. We listen to these voices, the attention wanders, and we inevitably conclude that this is just not the right time, the right place, the right way, the right me, to do what we set out to do.

Distraction (the constant conversation) is the ego-identity maintenance system playing the Wizard of Oz. Distraction diverts attention from the present to an illusory alternate reality.

There is no such thing as a harmless distraction. Any conversation is a diversionary tactic away from the moment.

We follow the distraction, and when we come to we realize that we have not meditated or gone to the gym. Now the problem is reframed as "something wrong with me" and the attention is diverted to what to do about me as the problem, since "I don't feel like it. I don't want to. I'll do it tomorrow."

With Awareness Practice, we begin to observe how not meditating happens. We can learn to recognize the sensations of distraction, see how it works, what it results in, and how it subtly (often not so subtly)

leads to suffering.

With practice, we come to the realization that in the absence of the conversation, in the absence of the distraction, there is no resistance to doing what we set out to do.

(If you hear a voice asking, "But what should I do about that?"...read on!)

STUDENT and SAGE #3

Student: I looked at what I get as the person who can't. What I saw is that I feel bad and kind of hopeless. If I can't do what I want to do, I'll never be able to have what I want.

Sage: What do you want? If you could meditate, if you could do the things that take care of you, what would you have? How would you be? How would you feel? Go home, watch carefully, see what arises. Come back and let me know.

To Get Past Resistance, We Have to Get Past Feeling Bad.

The payoff for not doing what the heart desires is that we feel bad. Feeling bad is the "proof" conditioning offers that "there's something wrong with you."

Let's look at how feeling bad happens.

1. It starts with a sense that there's something wrong with me. I'm overweight, I'm eating sugar again, the boss doesn't seem happy with me, I'm arguing with my partner, yelling at the kids...

Add your version of the same...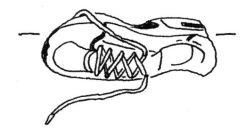

2. I decide to make a change. I go on a diet/exercise program; I commit to working harder and being even nicer.

30

3. Then I find I'm not keeping my commitment. I grab some ice cream as a treat because it was a hard day. I miss a workout. I feel annoyed with my boss. I feel tense, stressed, scared.

4. Soon I begin to feel bad because I'm not keeping to my program.

5. The conversation starts...

Here you go again. You'll never change. You are such a loser. Always have been. Always will be...

6. And, of course I believe it. How could I not? There's so much evidence--all those times I started and didn't keep up with what I said I'd do. It's true! There really is something wrong with me.

7. I feel
> terrible,
>> hopeless,
>>> despairing,
>>>> exhausted.

8. Then I think, "Well, maybe if I..." and I start down the road of figuring out what I need to do to fix it, to change me.

9. And the resistance starts to build...

10. I begin again at Step 1.

Self-hate
whipped me until I went
on a self-improvement program,
talked me out of staying with it,
and then beat me up for quitting.

Life has become a continuous
loop of feeling bad,
believing there is something wrong with me,
trying to be different,
committing to a program,
and failing.

If we look at this loop carefully,
we see that the payoff for feeling bad
is that it keeps the loop going.

My identity as a failure that can't (lose weight, get along with my partner, get to bed at a reasonable time, control my sugar/caffeine addiction, etc.) continues to be reinforced within this loop. As long as I am focused on feeling bad, I can never step back enough to see that I'm caught in a loop.

Feeling bad simply ensures that the ego-identity I'm conditioned to believe is "me" will be maintained.

We believe the voice that says, "I don't want to" and "I don't feel like it" (Step 4) is "me," just as we believe the voice that says, "You're a loser, there's something wrong with you" is telling the truth (Step 5).

The logic goes, "I hear it in my head, it sounds like 'me,' it must be me, it must be who I am." But we don't know that, do we?

What we don't ask is:
"Well, how do I know any of that is true?"
"Who says so?"
"What if it's not true?"

If we asked those questions, we would see that the internal voice of authority telling us what we're doing wrong and predicting failure is the very authority we consult to confirm that the judgments are true.

Consulting that false authority is a very bad idea!

Ego-I is a memory bank, a collection of stories of alleged mistakes and failures from the past, a continuous narrative that serves only to reinforce the illusion of a self that is separate from Life. We are conditioned to consult this narrative as the authority on who and what we are.

As long as our attention is on that conversation (I feel bad, I'm a failure, I can't do this) our Life experience IS the conversation.

We cannot have
the life we want
if we are unable
to drop the conversation
and be present to
Life as it is.

STUDENT and SAGE # 4

Student: I've realized that if I could do all the things I wanted to do (meditate, eat well, etc.), I'd feel good. I'd be relaxed and happy, but I'm afraid I'd never get anything done. Not only that, I think it would be  boring. And I'm pretty sure I couldn't keep it up anyway....

Sage: So you don't really want to meditate. Or to be happy?

Student: I do! But Life doesn't really work that way. Life is hard. It's not possible just to be relaxed and happy. I have to be realistic....

Sage: How do you know all that? What if that's not true? Doesn't it seem important to find out if what you believe is true?

Resistance: A point of view

The illusion of a separate self and the conditioned reality it inhabits are based on unexamined beliefs.

If we watch our reaction to anything we resist, we see that resistance arises from clinging to a point of view, a belief, or an assumption that's being challenged by what's arising in the moment.

For example, the unexamined belief that "Life is hard," results in a requirement to do all the hard things on the endless to-do list. Being caught in that loop reinforces the assumption that Life is indeed hard.

We're conditioned to believe that if we're happy and relaxed we'll be completely unprepared when things go wrong. And, besides, if we express how well things are going we'll be "tempting the devil." It's common to feel guilty or frightened about good fortune, feeling as if we have to compensate for it or deny it rather than simply being grateful for what we have.

Adversity, struggle, force, and will are all tools used in keeping the ego-identity maintenance system in good repair. Each is a form of resistance. If we drop the belief that these approaches are necessary to make things happen, we can have a direct experience of flowing with Life instead of resisting it.

Under the weight of a heavy snowfall pine boughs break, but by bending the willow can drop its burden and spring up again.
-- Zen saying

"Knowing" as Resistance

"In the beginner's mind there are many possibilities, in the expert's mind there are few."
-- Shunryu Suzuki Roshi

Knowing, in the sense of possessing knowledge, is an attempt to create a static reality. Believing we know strips the world of mystery and wonder and denies what Life is--fresh, new, dynamic--different in each moment.

 Can you remember a time when the whole world was a giant Exploratorium? A time of insatiable curiosity when we thought nothing of trying to stick our fingers into an electric socket to find out what's inside those little holes? As children we were gloriously alive to any possibility, living every day as an adventure, waking up in anticipation of what the day would bring, excited about and interested in everything. Over time curiosity, wonder, awe, and learning for the sheer joy of learning are conditioned out of us.

When I already "know" something, I don't need to be present; I don't need to be here to experience what's arising in this moment. I assume I already know what's here.

We miss Life when we believe that we already know. We miss Life when we believe we don't have to be present to have a direct experience of Life right now.

"I know" is an "expert" position
with egocentric karmic conditioning/self-hate
squarely in control of our lives.

"Not knowing"
is dangerous territory
for the ego-identity survival system.
"Not knowing" challenges
the beliefs and assumptions
underpinning ego's imaginary world.

Here are a few of the many ways by which we are discouraged from approaching Life with an open mind.

⇒ I already know that.

Ego-identity dismisses any information that challenges what it already "knows." For instance, I come across this piece of information: **Sugar and caffeine provide a temporary boost in energy but over time deplete energy.** Here's what tends to happen after the first two or three times I hear that. Ego-identity files that information in the "I already know that" category. What's being filed is the *recognition* of the information, not the **experience** of it. Yes, there is recognition of the words, but there is no inquiry, no exploration, no direct experience of the truth or falsity of the information.

AN ASIDE

You might recognize this phenomenon when ego-I encounters what it identifies as "repeated information" in this book. It doesn't grasp the meaning of what's being said, but, recognizing the words, bridles at what it calls "repetition."

⇨ I should know that.

I encounter something new, and instead of being excited to learn about it I shut

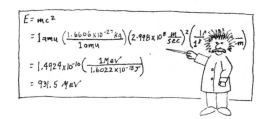

down in resistance. The resistance arises in the form of feeling bad that "I should already know about that." I become preoccupied with feeling bad, ashamed, humiliated, and stupid (all of which those voices in my head say about me with regularity). I close off to the opportunity of receiving the information that Life is freely offering me.

⇨ I have to get it right, and I only get one shot at it.

Many of us have the experience of being paralyzed when we make a commitment to start something new, even if we find it exciting. We're trained to resist anything that takes us

out of our comfort zone...

Since exploration and inquiry are discouraged, we don't realize that "outside of my comfort zone" refers to anything that would challenge the boundaries of the ego-identity within which we are doomed to live our lives.

We are told that we can't do something unless we do it right or do it well. It's not about finding out for ourselves. It's about meeting some vague standard of perfection.

I am drawn to painting. If my first attempt with a paintbrush doesn't produce the equivalent of a Van Gogh, I'm told I should give up. That's a slight exaggeration of course, but you get the picture! (Pun intended.)

We're not allowed to learn to do something new **because we don't already know how to do it!** Ego-I wants a guaranteed outcome before we start.

> We are so conditioned to believe we have to get an A before we take the class that we don't sign up for the class.

45

The thrill of learning
was left behind
with childhood.

Even worse, firmly believing we get only one shot at whatever we're attempting, we're rarely allowed to approach something new with the awareness that we will be **transformed in the process** of building a skill or competency.

⇨ Taking it personally instead of taking it in

Someone sees the dark circles under my eyes, asks if I'm getting enough sleep, comments about how important sleep is, and offers me advice on sleeping better.

The conditioned reaction is to feel criticized and to resist the input. I get defensive, feel judged, am offended, think people should mind their own business. Doing something to change our habit patterns, being open to finding out how it could be different, is rarely on the menu.

The result is that we are not present or open to the helpful suggestions that Life is offering, suggestions that could make a huge difference in our quality of Life.

We only "know" what conditioning tells us we know. To experience how Life works is to get past the resistance of the ego expert and let go into the "not knowing" of Life unfolding.

STUDENT and SAGE #5

Student: I've been looking at your "how do you know" question, and I've realized that I don't know. I see what you mean by the constant conversation in my head. It tells me all sorts of things and
I believe it. But I don't actually know that what I'm being told is true.

Sage: Can you see that the conversation is creating a world for you that not only may not be true, but also does not serve you?

Student: Well maybe, but...

Sage: There! Your "Well maybe, but..." is the resistance I'm talking about! That's the conversation you need to see. Where does that knee-jerk, automatic resistance come from?

Student (after a thoughtful moment): I don't know.

Sage: Perhaps it stems from facing the possibility that if the world the conversation is creating for you is not true or real, you don't know where that leaves you.

Resistance: The Voice of the Internal Authority

Cynicism, skepticism and negation are automatic reactions to alternatives that challenge conventional beliefs and assumptions. The reactions often sound like: No way! I don't believe it. That's crazy. Or the subtler but just as resistant, Yes but....

When we say we have "authority issues," we mean that we believe the story told by the internal voice that says "I have trouble with people who claim to be an authority on something. I don't trust them and I'm not going to get fooled by them." That story is a guarantee that the only authority I am allowed to listen to and follow is the voice in my head. Any suggestion that contravenes that internal authority meets my "authority issues" story head on.

I am working in the Monastery
kitchen cutting tomatoes.
Someone shows me an
alternative way to cut them..
I have cut tomatoes the

same way all my Life. I feel an instant flash of
resistance.

My automatic "no" reaction highlights my Lifelong,
unconscious habit of consulting a "reality" called "how
I've done it before" as the absolute authority for
how it "should" be done.

"It is your mind that creates this world."
-- The Buddha

Meditation is such an important aspect of Awareness
Practice because it allows us to have a direct
experience of how the mind creates the reality
we're living in. In meditation, it's possible to see
the processes of the conditioned mind--judging,
comparing, labeling, interpreting, abstracting,
rejecting--busily creating the world each of us
believes is real.

We also see the beliefs and assumptions that maintain "reality." For example, in my world people should be fair, it's wrong to tell lies, it's important to be in control, I need to have better hair, my aunt is mean, and my boss is perfect. It never occurs to me that no one else has the same internal experience of reality that I do. I take my reality as truth.

And, of course, we all know the experience of having other realities collide with ours. My aunt does something kind for me, my boss says something jerky, and I'm repeatedly told my hair is beautiful. Amazingly, the voices keep the same stories going, in spite of all the evidence contradicting them. Even more amazing is that I continue to believe them!

Being grounded in Awareness Practice is the most helpful way to approach all Life situations. I may want to have better relationships, be more successful at work, lose weight, quit smoking, exercise, meditate regularly--the content is endless and varied--

but I will never
have what I want
until I realize
how conditioning
creates a reality in which
I say I want one thing
and somehow end up
choosing the opposite.

STUDENT and SAGE #6

Student: At first I thought, "This is stupid! I need to stop talking to that sage." Then I had a terrifying thought: "What if it's true that the world I live in isn't real; what happens to me?" And, then something  extraordinary occurred to me. "If that world isn't real, if what I believe isn't true, maybe I'm not hopeless, maybe there isn't anything wrong with me." Then I heard, "But you still can't meditate."

Sage: Can you see that the conversation with all those unexamined beliefs and assumptions not only maintains a world, it maintains a "you," an ego-identity that inhabits that world?

Student: Yes, it's tricky to hold on to, but I can sort of see that.

Sage: That ego-identity "you" defines itself by what you are not. It is maintained by a focus on all that you "can't." To say it another way, the ego-identity is maintained by resisting what is. Go home now and meditate again and watch how the "I" is maintained.

The Big Fat Illusion

The most fundamental implication of the Sanskrit word "dukkha" (often translated as "suffering") is impermanence.

> Everything changes.
> Nothing is permanent.

"What we call a 'being,' or an 'individual' or 'I' according to Buddhist philosophy, is only a combination of ever-changing physical and mental forces or energy."
-- Walpola Rahula

Attachment to an idea of ourselves as a constant, permanent entity causes us to resist change, to resist Life, and to resist what we actually are.

Sadly,
we trade participating
wholeheartedly
in all of Life
to cling to a belief
that we are something
that does not exist.

In the words of Wei-Wu-Wei: "Why do we suffer? Because 99.9 per cent of everything we do is for the self. And there isn't one."

BIG FAT ILLUSION S·A·N·D·W·I·C·H

SESAME SEEDS OF ILLUSION

"I" cannot imagine a reality in which "I" does not exist.

"I" is a mental construct created moment by moment by the constant conversation of conditioned mind, which hijacks attention, dragging it into an imaginery past or rocketing it into an imaginery future-anything to avoid the present. Why? Because

NO NUTRITION

"I" cannot imagine a reality in which "I" does not exist! —

and "I" does not exist in the present.

The incessant conversation of conditioned mind assists in maintaining the idea of a permanent "I."

We must keep in mind that the point of the incessant conversation in the head is to distract attention from the present.

The reason for this is quite simple: the ego-identity does not, cannot, exist in the present. This is critical to realize.

We are tricked into avoiding the present through having our attention consumed by stories of an imaginary future or an imaginary past. The conversation is about anything other than what is actually unfolding herenow.

A typical ego-identity bamboozle: I'm not going to spend money on the things I'd enjoy now because I'm saving money to prevent a future I won't want. We are talked into missing the present to dread, or anticipate, imaginary events existing only in conditioned mind.

Another bamboozle: I am tortured by stories of past failures. I get tricked into giving up a perfectly fine **now** to watch scenes from a made up past. And, yes, it is a made up past, because what was recording what happened **then** was conditioning, and what is telling the story **now** is conditioning. The spin conditioning has put on "past" events is designed to be compelling enough to guarantee attention stays with the images and stories **and safely out of the present.**

"No deed there is, no doer thereof."
-- from the Upanishads

When attention is HERE in the moment, there's the ability to **be** movement, thought, and sensations without a "someone" thinking, moving, or feeling.

"O body swayed to music, O brightening glance, How can we know the dancer from the dance?"
-- W. B. Yeats

In identification
with the "I,"
there is an experience
of an experiencer
but not an experience
of Life.

The Negativity of I

The Sage says: The ego-identity "you" is maintained by a focus on all you "can't." It defines itself by what you are not. In other words, ego-identity is a negative process.

EGO MATH

$$EGO(LIFE) = \sim (LIFE)$$

The function EGO takes in
experience LIFE and
outputs NOT LIFE.

To maintain itself, the ego-identity must constantly reinforce what is NOT authentic being. The maintenance system is always focused on ensuring that we are not successful at what we set out to do; otherwise ego-identity ceases to exist. When we understand this, we can see how our attempts to overcome it rarely work.

This is best illustrated by an example:
I'm tired of being overweight and decide to go on a diet. I have tried many times to lose weight but have always failed. I believe it's my fault and I feel bad.

What's happening here? We are fooled into thinking that "I" actually want to lose weight. However, the ego-identity being maintained is: "I am overweight. I hate being overweight but there's nothing I can do about it." That identity will be maintained at any cost. Translation: You will be beaten over the issue for a Lifetime but you will NEVER lose weight. (And, of course, you'll be told it's your fault.)

THE OLD BAIT & SWITCH BAMBOOZLE

THE BAIT

Ego-1: This is how you look, but...

...this is how you should look.

PSH*: You're right. I'll eat less and exercise more.

THE SWITCH

Ego-1: You're exercising so much. You deserve a third slice of pizza. Eat more chocolate. Deprivation leads to failure. Your legs are tired. Exercise tomorrow.

PSH: Uh, ok, I guess that's right.

*Poor Suffering Human

In this scenario
I am engaged in an
ego maintenance program
not a weight loss program.

From the ego-identity maintenance perspective the person who wants to lose weight is always engaged in a process of WANTING to lose weight, not in a process of LOSING weight. It must always be a process of trying and failing because if I succeed and lose weight, **an ego-identity ceases to exist.**

A weight loss program from an ego-identity perspective is willpower, deprivation, guilt, blame, punishment, and self-hate--in short, anything that continues to makes us feel bad but does not affect the issue.

The only way to be successful
with any behavior change
that threatens the ego
is to cease to identify with the ego-I
that is maintaining itself
through maintaining the issue.

With practice we can step out of the ego-identity
process of
assessment,
judgment,
comparison,
evaluation,
and criticism.

We can stop believing "I should be different," and
we can begin to explore what we authentically **are**.

We can go from living in a world of "something
wrong with me" to being present and available to
Life as Life is.

From presence we can open to what is possible
when we pay attention to and honor what a human
being is and needs.

(To bring us back to weight loss, it's important to
tune in to what the body needs for its
nourishment rather than allowing the
ego to feed itself.)

"I want to but I can't"
is a problem in the world
of ego-identity.
It is not
a problem in Life.

STUDENT and SAGE #7

Student: That was amazing! While meditating, I saw all those same things --fidgeting, hating it, getting distracted, not wanting to, but I could see that the whole thing was a  non-stop effort to get me to quit. Then I saw something huge. That conversation is going on all the time, controlling what I think, what I say, what I do. And I'm starting to see it's not me. I am the one watching it!

Sage: Very good! You are seeing that you are not that system (the voices in your head and the feelings in your body) and that it resists anything that would allow you to **see that it is not you.** So here is your assignment: Now that you see it's a process that is not "you," watch to see the **how** of it. Look to see how that process works.

A Life-Stealing Story

"The 'I' is an imposter habitually swooping in, staking claim to experience."
-- from an email class participant

We know what the conventional sense of taking something personally is. Someone says something or something happens and I make it mean something about "me." Egocentric karmic conditioning/self-hate is a process of "taking Life personally."

Life unfolds. Right behind the arising of Life in the moment comes the meaning-making mechanism of conditioned mind. This split-second-after-the-moment interpretation of what's arising creates the illusion of a "someone" experiencing Life.

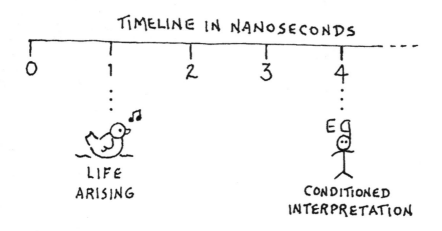

TIMELINE IN NANOSECONDS

0   1   2   3   4

LIFE
ARISING

CONDITIONED
INTERPRETATION

We offered in *When You're Falling, Dive* the following explanation of how the illusion of that someone is created.

First, there's **movement** (the constant flux of the universe). Then there's **sensation** (when the body's senses register the movement). A second later ego-I comes in to make meaning out of what arose by attaching a label to the sensation. This label usually takes the form of a **thought** about the sensation. The thought is followed by an **emotional reaction**, which in turn is followed by a karmically conditioned **behavior** (what we believe needs to be done about what we feel).

If we are present at the moment of Life unfolding, we have a choice to follow the habitual story/interpretation or to keep attention in the present. If attention follows the story, we are not paying attention to what is and we are not available to have

a direct experience of Life.

If we are not HERE
as the moment unfolds,
we are doomed to a secondary,
interpreted-by-karmic-conditioning
existence.

When we are identified with ego-identity
we are not actually living Life--
we're living a Life-stealing story
about Life.

There's Nothing Wrong, and...

There is nothing inherently wrong with a conditioned reaction. There's nothing wrong with egocentric karmic conditioning/self-hate. There's nothing WRONG with anything!

Suffering doesn't make us bad.
Ending suffering doesn't make us good.
(One process does not lead to another.)
If I'm suffering it just means I'm suffering.
If I'm not suffering it just means I'm not suffering.
Actually it doesn't even mean that!
If I'm suffering, I'm suffering.
If I'm not suffering, I'm not suffering.
None of it MEANS anything!

One of the best things about what the Buddha taught is that it's all our choice. We can drop all notions of right/wrong, good/bad--the dualistic world of illusion maintained by the imaginary separate self. Then Awareness Practice becomes simple and obvious: **We now can be what we want to have.** Listening to voices argue about right and wrong, good and bad, is a waste of our precious time.

Christmas Humphreys said,
"We are punished
by what we do,
not because of it."

Given that, it's up to us to choose the life we
want to have,

and then to have it.

Attending to the Life We Want

The inevitable consequence of social conditioning is a survival system that once represented safety but over time has become a prison. To question or challenge what we've been taught to believe since before we can remember feels dangerous; to let it go feels like non-survival.

In Awareness Practice, we are going up against that survival system. And it mightily resists our efforts.

Our way past that resistance lies in our ability to direct attention to thisherenow.

Conditioned mind runs on fear and anxiety, based in conditional "realities" in which bad and good are measured out and should be balanced. But it's all illusion. Life simply is. We miss our opportunity to BE with Life when we give attention to the meaning-making mechanism of ego-identity's labeling and interpreting. When we believe the meanings conditioning attaches to what is, when we engage with the conversation in our heads that maintains those meanings, we struggle in a dualistic world filled with bad and good, attempting to cling to pleasure and avoid pain.

Here, in the present, there is Life as is, and there's nothing wrong with any of it.

STUDENT and SAGE #8

Student: So I sat down and
had a couple of good
moments. Then I heard,
"This doesn't feel right,"
quickly followed by "You're
not meditating." Then I

wondered, "What should it feel like? How do I know
what it feels like to meditate? In fact, who would
know?"

Sage: This is good to see. Are you recognizing a
subtler form of resistance here? Can you see the
comparison of what is--you meditating--to a belief
that there's a way it "should" or "could" be? The
message is, "If it doesn't feel like it should, you're
not doing it right." Attention is turned away from
"just meditating" and toward conditioned mind's story
about what isn't the way it should be, how what is
should be different from the way it is.

Student: Not sure I can see it: I can sort of sense
that's what happens.

Sage: Good. The process of resistance "**wants something other than what is.**" This is a universal process; it's not personal. As long as you believe that something should be different than it is, you are identified with the process of resistance. Most of the time we unconsciously go along with what resistance is saying and doing, so we never experience it as resistance. Nothing is flagging us as unusual so we just experience it as "me" living "my" Life, making "my" decisions.

Student: Well, you're right about that. It does feel like me.

Sage: So here's what I want you to do next. Do something that you know there will be resistance to. Don't make it something big--drink tea instead of coffee for example--and watch what happens.

Losing Interest in How "I" Feels

Losing interest in how "I" feels is a powerful way to practice being present to what is.

LOOK INTO MY EYES...
YOU ARE GETTING SLEEPY...
YOU ARE FEELING ANXIOUS,
FRIGHTENED, CONFUSED
AND MISERABLE...

"How I feel" often dictates what we do. If I'm feeling lazy, I don't go out for the run I planned. If I'm feeling tired, I'm easily talked out of meditating. If something feels hard, I feel justified in procrastinating.

All kinds of "unpleasant" sensations lie beneath "I don't feel like it." The sensations themselves are not actually unpleasant, but they've been labeled unpleasant because the stories associated with them are dread, discomfort, worry, anxiety, fear of failure, fear of uncertainty, anticipation of difficulty...

We're conditioned to avoid those sensations; we've learned to retreat when we feel them arise. Over time we're trained to withdraw from situations that present even a slight possibility of those sensations being triggered. We learn to choose what feels like alternatives to the discomfort associated with the sensations, believing the stories that avoidance means we'll be safe and feel okay.

Examples:
-- Someone says something objectionable but it feels uncomfortable to point that out, so I don't.
-- My boss asks me to do something that I don't agree with, but I don't stand up for myself, fearing consequences.
-- I've just come home from a really hard day at work, and I'm told I'd rather sit on the couch than make the effort to get to the dance class I signed up for, even though I know from past experience I'll feel better if I dance.

For most people, "I don't feel like it" is a constant, invisible barrier of resistance. We encounter the barrier, and we're stopped from moving forward with our intention. We fall back into old, familiar, often suffering-producing, self-hate reinforcing patterns of behavior. We get bamboozled into going with a belief (I can't do this), an assumption (it's too hard), an opinion (it's not that important), and an identity (I'm just shy/weak/a coward/a loser) that's keeping ego safe--at our expense!

KEEPING EGO SAFE

Belief— I can't.

Assumption— It's too hard.

Opinion— It's not important.

Identity— I'm a loser.

As soon as we get near an identity boundary, a "crusty layer," we begin to hear subtle messages of resistance. "This isn't how it should feel." "This is not an experience you want to have." We move from being present to the sensations in the body to being in conditioned mind:

1) assessing what is
2) comparing it to what should be
3) moving into the illusion of how it needs to be different.

We move from
being in Life

to being in a story
in conditioned mind.

Here are examples of conditioned messages that take us out of our authentic experience.

⇒ I'm told I'm a fraud, making it up, faking it if I'm having any experience other than the one ego says I should be having.

⇒ The environment has to be perfect, I have to feel exactly right, people have to be supportive, I have to finish everything on the to-do list. Then I can relax and be happy.

⇒ I can't be angry. I have to control my emotions and cannot say what's going on for me. If I do get angry, I'm overcome with remorse and guilt for having lost control of my emotions.

⇒ My pet dies. I'm told it is unnatural to grieve over an animal and I need to get over it.

Add your version of the same...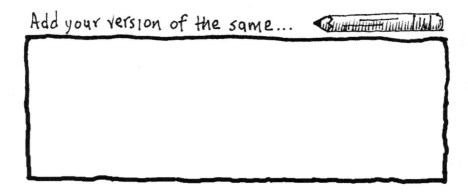

When we stay with sensations that ego-identity labels "unpleasant" or "uncomfortable," we have a radically different experience. We might recognize "I'm feeling depressed" as merely low energy, rather than something wrong and painful that needs to be avoided at all costs.

Anger can be experienced and consciously expressed as a state of high energy, instead of something shameful that needs to be suppressed.

Labels and the meaning attached to them distract us. We turn attention to the conditioned story of "I feel that and that means that and so I should do that," which takes us out of the moment. Without realizing what's happening, we choose conditioned beliefs (anger is bad, depression must be avoided) over our ability to be present with Life as it unfolds.

We can learn to experience
the full spectrum
of sensations and emotions
available to us
in healthy,
Life-affirming ways.

STUDENT and SAGE #9

Student: I took on your suggestion to drink tea instead of coffee. I didn't want to. What I heard was "I need coffee, I'll never make it, I hate this." And then I watched

"resolve and determination" kick in: "this is the right thing to do and I'll make myself do it regardless," which has never worked. I'm seeing that throughout my Life I've tried to use resistance to accomplish my heart's desire.

Sage: So, what do you see about that?

Student: I suspect that whole process is the source of misery rather than the route to happiness.

Sage: Yes! Now you are ready to explore the alternative. The desire to meditate comes from a different level of consciousness than the ego-identity survival system of resistance. Maintaining this new level of consciousness requires changing behaviors that have held the survival system in place.

There Is No Change in Consciousness without a Change in Behavior.

Realizing that resistance is a process is not enough to get us to change our conditioned orientation as the "I" of ego.

We act out our karmic identities by default.

To drop an identity we must change the behaviors associated with it. As we have seen, the defenses ego-identity has in place to prevent that from happening are formidable.

Here is an example: Say I grew up in a family where strong emotions were never expressed. I received messages that even saying what was going on for me was not a good survival plan. The right-person-thing-to-do was to hide my feelings and not communicate what was going on for me. The result? I became really good at suppressing what I feel. I have a lifetime of stuffing my feelings, I live in a pressure cooker of emotional resentment, but no one else can tell there's anything going on.

Of course, even an expert such as I in emotion stuffing has limits. Eventually the resentment builds  until that last straw is piled on. I explode, spewing out all that hurt and anger, saying things I later regret. I feel awful, guilty. I'm desperate to make it up to those I've hurt and offended. I resolve to become better at controlling myself, more adept at hiding my emotions.

Pressure builds.

At some future date I don't keep that promise.

Repeat the loop.

What I don't see
is that the original conditioning was bogus,
and that the best way out of the loop
is to express what I feel.

Not expressing what I feel maintains the loop. Practicing expressing what I feel is the behavior change that will free me of the identity that keeps me in suffering. The behavior change invalidates the assumption that ego-I is keeping alive.

As we practice working with resistance, we need to identify the behavior change that will invalidate ego's bogus stories.

The Difference between Behavior and Being

Now here's the tricky part. A suggestion that I communicate more--from, say, a trusted friend-- makes me defensive. Instead of hearing a request for a change in behavior, I hear criticism of who I am. I hear judgment that something is wrong with me, and that I should change.

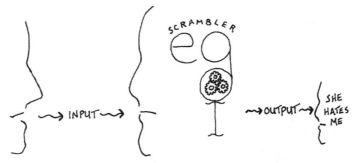

In other words, information that might be helpful is interpreted by the fearful identity as a threat to its survival (which it is!). It takes it all very personally. I feel bad, I feel criticized, and I'm not a bit open to receiving more information that could change my Life experience for the better.

Conditioning keeps us from realizing
there's a difference--
as vast as our experience of the difference
between suffering and freedom--
between "who" a person is as ego-identity
and "what" a person is authentically.

The ego survival system is well served by people not being able to tell the difference between the two.

We're exploring the difference between authentic nature and the survival system of ego-identity, or the difference between being and behavior. I get very defensive, nearly aggressive, if I feel accused. That defensiveness is the ego survival system created in childhood to protect "me" that's now protecting itself. If I realize the difference, I will begin to see how those two processes manifest and what the result of each is in my life.

Resistance as Resistance

Looking at the "how" of resistance allows us to see it for what it is. In *seeing* it we disidentify from it, stepping back into the process of seeing rather than the process of resisting. As long as we are identified with resistance, the only way we have to overcome it is by resisting it, which keeps us squarely in resistance.

Developing the ability to "notice" resistance—not taking it personally, not feeling bad about it, not trying to fix it, not attempting to get rid of it—allows us to **be in Life** rather than resisting Life. The present, Life, is the only "place" from which it is possible simply to notice.

We cannot be hurt or surprised that the ego maintenance system does all it can to ensure its survival. That's just how it works. Our task is to develop the escape velocity required to get beyond the gravitational field of ego-identity maintenance.

It takes practice. We are so conditioned to identify with the ego, with that illusion of a "someone" outside of Life, that it can feel impossible to develop an alternate way of being. But it's not.

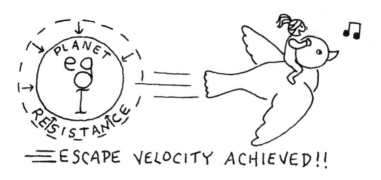

≡ESCAPE VELOCITY ACHIEVED!!

The Buddha taught that ignorance of the nature of Life, of our true nature, maintains suffering. When we awaken, identification with the ego as the only reality vanishes. The good news is that we're already in Life; we're "being" all the time. We just don't always know it--yet.

The change in behavior that we practice to get past resistance is **disidentification**. Awareness Practice is the practice of disidentification. We develop the ability to stop identifying with the process that creates and maintains the "I" of ego. We learn to lose interest in the story of "something wrong and not enough" being maintained by the voices of egocentric karmic conditioning/self-hate. We step out of the process of resistance into being the awareness that sees how it works. We learn to direct our attention to thisherenow, to Life as it is unfolding in the moment.

FORMS OF RESISTANCE

Exchanges between Student and Sage
as the Student Explores Resistance

It's Hard to Be Present.

Student: Practice feels like a long, hard road. It feels like I have to make such an effort to be present. It's hard to get past the resistance of "It's too hard, I don't want to."

Sage: Yes, the voices put forth the idea that Life should be easy and Nirvana and everything that ego pretends to want should be obtained with no effort! How silly.

I just want to be happy.
I don't want to.
pick up after the kids.
Why can't I be rich
and pay someone
to do everything?

I don't want
to clean
the house.

Why can't I just
be peaceful?

I don't feel
like going
to work.

Why do I have
to meditate?

I don't want to "pay attention."

We're taught to hold conflicting beliefs that 1) we shouldn't have to work at anything and 2) we have to urgently strive in busyness and stress or we will never get what we want. Then we're meant to conclude that the effort required simply to **be** present in Life is just too hard. The truth is it takes no effort to be present; it is utterly restful to be in Life.

Student: So, how long will it take to work through all my conditioning?

Sage: When we begin Awareness Practice, it is necessary to learn to recognize egocentric karmic conditioning/self-hate in whatever forms it takes. We sit in meditation and become familiar with ego's shenanigans, simply observing it as it does

what it does. In this way it becomes clear that ego-identity is the conditioned response to whatever arises in life, and that it is absolutely devoted to suffering. However, it is not necessary to completely chip away the layers of karmic conditioning or to dismantle the ego to have an authentic Life. Once we are adept at recognizing its tactics, we stop engaging with it.

We learn to turn attention away from it and to the Life experience we want to be having in any given moment. This process is simple and easy, because in practice we are not becoming something new and different. We are turning the attention to what we authentically are and always have been.

The only thing making Life hard is our unhealthy relationship with egocentric karmic conditioning/self-hate.

Remember, a change in consciousness requires a change in behavior. A moment of authentic behavior that accurately expresses Life is transformative. We maintain the change in consciousness by practicing the change in behavior. That change is what ego-I resists.

Student: The behavior change then proves that the identity being maintained is false, right? So, if the identity being maintained is "practice is too hard for me," and I practice anyway, I'll see that the identity is false and be free of it.

Sage: Exactly so. You will be free of it in that moment.

Resistance to Repetition

Student: A new schedule of retreats at the Monastery has been posted. I've done all the retreats before and feel resistance to signing up for something I've done already. The voices tell me I know what will happen and am not going to learn anything new.

Sage: What are you seeing about that?

Student: There's a belief that for something to be worthwhile it has to be new and different. If it's something I've done before, there's nothing new to learn. Repetition is pointless and boring.

Repetitious and Boring Things I Have Done Before

- EAT
- SLEEP
- BREATHE
- MOVE
- TALK
- READ
- PLAY

Sage: Have you noticed how repetitive, predictable, boring, and singularly lacking in originality the voices of resistance are? And yet we listen to them as if our lives hung in the balance!

In the present, nothing ever repeats.
"Past" is an illusion.
There is no "before,"
just as there is no "next."
There is only now.
This moment is new, you are new, everything is new.

"Sameness" is an attribute of conditioned mind, not of Life.

Student: So you're saying that I get talked out of doing something that would allow me to have a direct experience that Life is never the same from moment to moment?

Sage: Yes. Resistance to repetition is really resistance to Life.

Hope as Resistance

Student: I'm always hoping that when I sit down to meditate I'll feel peaceful. It's true I sometimes get to a place of peace, but then I find myself thinking about the possibility of feeling peaceful all the time.

Sage: Good to see, yes? Hope is not what enables us to see what's possible; our authentic nature IS what's possible--that's how we can be aware of possibility.

Hope, peace, joy, love, goodness, gratitude... as **ideas** are illusion. We never feel peace when we're chasing conditioned mind's idea of peace. When we chase an idea, we feel only the dissatisfaction of comparing our experience to conditioned mind's version of what we should or could feel.

Wonderfully, peace, wellbeing, and harmony await us when we are in Life, flowing with Life, in thisherenow, with whatever is arising.

Ideas about hope and possibilities
are ruses conditioning uses
to ensure attention is not on the
peace of oneness
with the present moment.

Resistance to Committing

Student: I was asked to make a practice commitment in a recent email class with Cheri. The encouragement I received when I sent in my response was to commit to something specific instead of stating a vague intention. I confess to feeling both irritated and angry at the response.

Sage: You can see what was actually irritated and angry, can't you?

Student: Yes. Ego-I was irritated because someone saw through what it was trying to do. Conditioning wants to make the whole thing sufficiently abstract so that I don't have anything I'm actually practicing.

Sage: Very good. When we make a commitment to something as vague, say, as "be kinder," conditioning can take charge of defining what that means. Conditioning decides what being kind is, if and when I'm kind, whether I'm being kind enough and so forth.

There is so much more scope to practice kindness if I make a commitment such as: I will take 15 minutes each morning to be kind to my body by doing X. Conditioning will do everything in its power to ensure that does not happen! There will be tremendous resistance to keeping such a simple, specific practice commitment because in seeing how I am able to keep the commitment or how the voices prevent me from keeping it, every aspect of the path to liberation will be revealed.

No wonder specific commitments are resisted so strenuously by conditioned mind.

Overwhelm as Resistance

Student: I run into a lot of situations in which I feel overwhelmed with what I'm asked to do. It feels like there's a very young part of me who becomes teary and sad because she can't face the situations she's put into. She's the one who doesn't want to and doesn't feel like doing most things, and who could blame her? I've tried to reassure her but I keep encountering her resistance. She just refuses.

Sage: That young part of you needs to be embraced in compassion and allowed to be the child she is. She doesn't need to be out front, coping with overwhelming situations.

It is important to remember that any "part of ourselves" that does not want to be healed is not authentic. No "real child" caught in the pain of childhood trauma will choose to stay stuck in that trauma when present moment love and acceptance is offered.

Student: I think you're saying that the "overwhelm," the feeling of "I don't want to and I won't," is egocentric karmic conditioning/self-hate masquerading as a small child aspect of the personality. Right?

MASTER MASQUERADER

Sage: Exactly. Egocentric karmic conditioning is adept at adopting any form in order to stay in the spotlight. It would refuse compassion so that your attention can be focused on it as both a "wounded child" and a "loving adult."

Ego gets to play out a childish orientation to Life, the ultimate place of resistance where "I" has absolute control, and "I" lives in the story that I don't have any control because nothing is "my" fault. "I" gets to be the victim.

In that victim stance, "I" doesn't have to take responsibility. It's never "my" fault. I can feel sorry for myself and stay overwhelmed. I never have to grow up.

Student: I guess I fell for that ego-scam. I've believed authentic being is a small child that has been traumatized and must be nurtured back to health.

Sage: Ego scams are always good to see and see through. We need to remember that the work we are doing is to be unconditional love, offering compassion for all.

"I Don't Want To, You Can't Make Me" as Resistance

Student: I often have this reaction when I encounter someone who suggests something that is good for me. I immediately go to "I don't want to and you can't make me." When I started through the checklist of sensations, thoughts, emotions and so forth, I realized I was feeling the way I felt when I was a teenager. Not the self-conscious, shy adolescent I was sometimes, but the surly, angry, hostile kid. I was sick to death of people telling me what to do, making me do things I didn't want to do, giving me "advice," putting their interests and values on me. I wanted to have my own life, do what I wanted. I could feel it in my body, and the conversation was colorful to say the least.

Sage: Very good. You've seen something important about how conditioning takes advantage of vulnerable aspects of a person's personality--in this case an unsure adolescent--to act out resistance. When a person takes the bait and identifies with the subpersonality, he or she believes that subpersonality is their authentic being. A person seeing the world through that personality's eyes readily does the bidding of conditioning.

The personality does not need pity or grieving or anger about what happened. The personality needs compassionate acceptance NOW and will happily be embraced into a loving, accepting present.

Student: So you're not suggesting I turn attention away from that kid and put it where I choose it to be?

Sage: No. That child did not have someone with the ability to listen, reflect, understand, and hold up a compassionate mirror. So the child has remained stuck, wisely, until that compassion is available.

Student: Wisely?

Sage: Yes. In spite of tremendous pressure to abandon ourselves, we refuse. We dig in and stay stuck right there until the compassion that can set us free comes along. Very intelligent, don't you think?

Student (laughing): Well, it certainly puts a different light on "stubbornly clinging."

Sage: It does. We must keep in mind that there's nothing wrong with anything. And, we must learn to discern if we are experiencing the tenacity of someone clinging to a life raft in a fierce storm or the resistance of egocentric karmic conditioning/self-hate trying to talk us into giving up!

Fear as Resistance

Student: I've been looking at fear as resistance. It seems to me that at the root of anything I resist is fear--fear of failure, fear of outcomes, fear of the unfamiliar--all different disguises and colors of fear. In fact I've watched myself being afraid of feeling afraid.

Sage: This is very important to see, isn't it? As we've been discussing, ego-identity is an imaginary boundary that marks "I/me/mine" as separate.

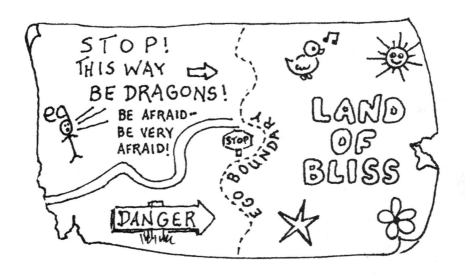

"Fear" is the sensations of resistance we feel when we push against the boundary and come close to experiencing what is **beyond** ego, what **contains** ego. Fear is successful in defending the boundary because we're conditioned to be afraid of feeling fear and to avoid it.

Staying with the sensations reveals them to be nothing to be afraid of--merely sensations erroneously labeled. Breathing through them carries us beyond the boundary into a direct experience of all that's beyond ego-identity.

Student (smiling): So resisting being afraid is not what we're going for?

Sage: Correct. We want to learn to stay present to the sensations, then we can move beyond what conditioned mind has labeled as fear.

Anxiety as Resistance

Student: Is anxiety the same as fear?

Sage: Anxiety is an ego-I resistance to presence. Anxiety, worry, and expectation are all ways by which conditioning traps the attention to maintain its illusory world.

The faculties of memory and discrimination make it possible for a person to "remember" something in the past and project that into the future as something to be clung to or avoided. For instance, the last time I drank coconut water it had gone bad.

Now each time the possibility of drinking coconut water arises, revulsion to drinking it also arises. This maintains a constant "reality" against what is so currently.

We constantly receive messages that the world is something to be afraid of, leaving us coiled tightly in anxiety, imprisoned by the small world of "I." Identifying with the contraction, we are unable to experience the expansiveness that is Life.

Life is like a melody. The notes and the spaces between make up the song. When ego-I clings to the note, fearing its absence in the space, we don't get to experience ourselves as the song, just the contraction of a note afraid of the space.

Student: I like that. We are the melody, space and note, and each of us is a unique song. Nothing to be anxious about. Nothing to resist.

"Do I Deserve It?" as Resistance

Student: I am aware of all I've received from Life. Often, in the midst of feeling gratitude, I hear that I don't deserve what I have and I feel anxious. It's that waiting for the other shoe to drop place, waiting for it all to be taken away.

Sage: Yes, instead of accepting the abundance of Life, conditioning talks us into resisting it. The truth is, we don't deserve to be happy, nor do we  deserve to be unhappy. Life simply is. Life gives. It's like the weather. We classify it as bad or good and ascribe meaning based on how we feel about it, but it's just the weather. As with everything else in Life, it's not personal.

Do I
deserve
abundance?

"Deserving"
is an irrelevant concept.

Resistance to Impermanence

Student: For the past couple of days, I've been brimming over with insight. I feel like I'm dancing with Life and becoming aware of new ways of being. It feels wonderful.

Sage: I sense a "but..."

Student: I'm afraid it won't last, that I'll lose it and go back to suffering. I want to live like this all the time. The resistance I feel now is resistance to going back to a Life where ego rules.

Sage: Before practice, we are primarily unconscious and operating in conditioning's world, perhaps with brief, occasional glimpses of other possibilities.

Then we wake up to the possibility of living in the present, in insight.

As we become more skillful at directing attention, we become aware of the movement of attention

between Life and conditioned mind and we experience
that oscillation.

LIFE

CONDITIONED MIND

MOVEMENT BETWEEN LIFE

AND

(CONDITIONED MIND)

LIFE SAYS

NO REASON TO BE AFRAID

ACCEPT

NO COMPARING

NO MISTAKES

BE KIND TO YOURSELF

RIGHT HERE RIGHT NOW

NO RESISTANCE

NOTHING WRONG

LOVE

ENJOY!

CONDITIONED MIND SAYS

SOMETHING WRONG NOT ENOUGH YOU SHOULD NOT ENOUGH YOU SHOULD NOT ENOUGH SOMETHING WRONG NOT ENOUGH SOMETHING WRONG YOU SHOULDN'T SOMETHING WRONG YOU SHOULD NOT ENOUGH YOU SHOULDN'T SOMETHING WRONG YOU SHOULDN'T SOMETHING WRONG YOU SHOULD SOMETHING WRONG NOT ENOUGH

Student: So what I hear you saying is that I'm experiencing Life, then turning to conditioned mind to see how it's going, allowing my attention to move back and forth. I've had that experience enough to know where it leads!

Sage: Yes. It is important to see that practice **contains** that oscillation. The moment we feel resistance, clinging to insight, we can know we have moved away from insight. The only way to stay in insight is to stay in insight. **This is why learning to direct the attention is so important.**

The more we allow attention to be pulled towards the voices, the more momentum we build towards the ego orientation of conditioned mind.

Student: And that's what conditioning wants, yes?

Sage: Exactly. Conditioning will tell you it is inevitable you won't stay in insight. It says you can't do that--you never have--what makes you think you can do it now? But everything is changing all the time. So attention has to be with awareness all the time. It's not a one-time event, it's a lifetime endeavor and it takes a lifetime of practice. You are in training to realize you are being lived by Life. And you're learning that awareness is the process of living, the process of Life.

Student: Wait. That feels important.

Sage: It is! By practicing not being in conditioning, not giving attention to conditioning, we are in Life, having a **Life** experience.

We transcend conditioned mind,
we do not resist it.

Resistance to Guidance

Student: I've been looking at resistance to guidance and I think I see something really important. I was in the throes of extreme identification with ego. It was pointed out to me that I was identified with ego and was given guidance on what I could be looking at instead. I felt tremendous resistance to receiving the guidance. I felt humiliated and ashamed and was really angry that the person who offered the guidance made me feel small and vulnerable. I felt so exposed!

Sage: Guidance is having a mirror held up so we can stop being confused about what is ego-identity and what is authenticity. Because mirroring reveals conditioning in all of its ugliness, it is the process conditioning most resists.

UGLINESS OF EGO

CLEAR MIRROR

In the situation that you just described, it was the ego-I that felt threatened and small and humiliated and exposed. It **was** exposed; that is true.

The person offering guidance is not confused about what is authentic nature and what is the conditioned system.

The greatest gift we can receive is the ability to see what we are **not** so we can "realize" what we **are**.

Student: Yes. What I see now is how important it is to have ego identification mirrored. If I see what it is and what it does, I have the best chance of stepping away from it. I can see how it controls my life, and I can let it all go because it's **not ME!**

Sage: Yes. That's the single most important, and most difficult, thing to understand.

Egocentric karmic conditioning/self-hate
is <u>not</u>
what we are.

As long as we believe we are the small ego-I, we stay in ignorance and suffering. When we realize we are not that, we stop defending it, we stop worrying about how it makes us feel, and we open ourselves to authenticity.

EGO SAYS	LIFE SAYS	"MY" DEFENSE
You should be more disciplined.	Present moment compassion is the key.	But it's too hard to always be present.
You don't have enough time.	There is time. Stress doesn't help.	But if I relax I won't get anything done.
You are not attractive enough.	You are perfect as you are.	But nobody else thinks I am.
You should be more generous.	Start with being generous with yourself.	But I might become self-indulgent.

ADD YOUR OWN

Comparison as Resistance

Student: I'm looking at the process of resistance around receiving compliments. When someone says something nice or compliments me on what I've done, I usually dismiss it. Compliments embarrass me. When someone says I'm unique or special in some way, I find myself thinking, really? I'm not exceptional, not all that smart or talented. I want to believe it, but I don't. There's too much evidence to the contrary.

Sage: Well, that's not an accident. We are trained to believe the negative things the voices of judgment and self-hate say to and about us, and we are equally well trained not to receive anything that acknowledges our goodness.

The ego-I is constantly looking for better than or worse than because it's trying to maintain the illusion of separateness.

It does that through made-up, imaginary comparisons. Julie is prettier than Beth, but not nearly as pretty as Ann. Bob is more successful than Alan but Jane is more successful than either. (Did I mention they're all more attractive and successful than I am? Well, maybe not Beth... Hmmm... I'm not really sure about Alan...). And, so it goes, endlessly comparing, assessing, judging, competing, separating, isolating.

Comparison exists only in the imaginary dualistic world of egocentric karmic conditioning, in the world of "something wrong" and "not enough." It does not exist in authenticity.

Student: How is that so?

Sage: No two forms of Life are the same. All of Life is sacred. As we like to phrase it, everything is the Buddha. We are, each and all, divine expressions of Life, and Life is big enough to contain us as we are!

The belief that we should meet ego-I's standards keeps us from finding out that we are unique and perfect exactly as we are. How do we know we are perfect as we are? Because we are as we are.

Remember, this is it. There is no alternate reality where we are as ego-identity says we should be. And, it is essential that we find out how and what we are beyond ego-identity.

Student: So, if I'm following along here, appreciation is a Life process while comparing and judging is an ego process.

Sage: Yes! We have the opportunity to live every moment in appreciation of Life as it is (which is, by the way, a great definition of "joy.")

Liking and Disliking as Resistance

Student: Looking at appreciation brought me to wonder about acceptance. Should we just accept everything as is? There are a lot of things I don't want to accept. Especially negative things. I don't want to hear bad news, I don't like being around critical people who complain all the time. But then, I'm also aware that I get really irritated when someone (my Pollyanna sister!) wants to look only at the positive side of things and is unwilling to talk about or deal with what may be unpleasant.

Sage: We are conditioned to believe that what is pleasant is "positive" and positive is good, while what is unpleasant is "negative" and negative is not good. But that division is just another artifact of ego-I's dualistic fabrication.

Acceptance, as we describe it, does not exist in the world of ego-I. (Ego's dualistic process is either condemning or condoning. In conditioning's world, acceptance equals approval and breeds passivity.)

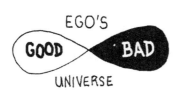

Acceptance is a process, an orientation to Life, not a judgment about the content of Life. Conditioned liking and disliking has no bearing on what IS, except that indulging dualistic thinking makes a life one of suffering.

Life contains everything, the entire range of human emotion, all orientations, all experiences, and every perspective. The joy of living comes from

acceptance of what IS and from willingness for
Life's impulse to move us as Life moves us.

Agonizing Over Decisions as Resistance

Student: I've been agonizing over a decision about
whether or not to take a
new job I've been offered.
I don't want to make the
wrong decision. What if I
don't like the job?

Sage: Remember, duality is a process of separating
Life into artificial pairs of opposites, and
"right/wrong" is a pair that ego loves to delude
people into agonizing over.

Student: So it makes no sense to
agonize over decisions? There is no
right and wrong?

Sage: Well, regardless of the amount of
agonizing, there is only the decision that
gets made.

Ego-I establishes a belief in right and wrong. It purports that it is possible to make the "right" decision, guaranteeing that things will go "the way I want." So we agonize and suffer over making the right decision.

> The fact of the matter
> is that it's not possible
> to make a bad decision.

If you take that job (move, buy that car rather than the other one, end your relationship, start a relationship, buy X, Y, or Z), and you hate it, you can always do something else. We get lost in the byways of our beliefs about whether it's ok to change, how long we should stay with the current, what if what we choose next is worse, etc.

> And the one and only point
> of the whole conversation
> is to keep a human being in suffering!
> Why?
> Because human suffering
> keeps the imaginary world of ego
> appearing real.

Student: Does that mean we should just give up and trust fate?

Sage: Dropping the right/wrong conversation and trusting Life does not mean "giving up" or "trusting fate." Dropping the conversation simply means we are available to the Wisdom and Intelligence that animate us to navigate whatever is arising. Our questions and the answers to our questions arise together.

> We practice presence
> to receive the information we need
> to live fully.

If I Am, I Cannot Do: Resistance to Being

Student: In the world that I live and work in effort is rewarded, striving means having purpose, success is defined as achievement and belonging is defined in terms of accomplishment. It's what I **do** that counts.

Sage: Yes, the belief that nothing can be accomplished without effort from ego-I shows up in awareness practice as "being present means we won't get anything done."

Action and presence are believed to be mutually exclusive, but that is an ego/identity fabrication, a story **about** Life. And, it's simply not true. It's perfectly possible to be present in action, even in intense action, because **Life is always the actor** regardless of what ego says!

Life is dynamic movement, coming into and going out of appearance.

Life creates anew in each moment: trees grow, canyons are carved, continents move. When we are present, we are part of the process of creation. There is no ego/identity separate from that.

Resistance prevents us from realizing we **are** Life movement. When we practice presence, ego-identity does not/cannot exist. It's no surprise that it resists any experience that challenges its existence.

Student: Yes. I can see that. In fact the most dominant message I hear when there is nothing to do is, "I'm bored. This is boring. I hate this." I am so afraid of being bored.

Sage: "Bored" is what ego/identity screams when nothing is reflecting it, when nothing is making it appear to be real. There is such intense resistance to anything that allows us to be in the present because, remember, in the present, ego does not/cannot, exist. The closer we get to being **here**, the sleepier or more bored we are told we are.

Meditation is the best place to embrace boredom. As the Zen saying goes: "If something is boring after two minutes, try it for four. If still boring, try it for eight, sixteen, thirty-two, and so on. Eventually, one discovers that it is not boring but **very** interesting."

Resistance as "Not Enough Time"

Student: I have been looking some more at doing and being. I live in a perpetual state of urgency and stress. There is so much to do and so little time to do it.

Sage: Life moves at its own rhythm. If we see our lives through the lens of what IS, then what gets done, gets done, what happens, happens. We must keep in mind there's no parallel reality in which what the voices say should or could happen is happening.

Student: As you say that, it occurs that my relationship with time causes me soooo much suffering. Time feels oppressive. My relationship with it is almost adversarial. There's not enough of it. I have to compete for it. I kill it! I'm sorry when I waste it. And yet when there's unscheduled time, like when I'm on retreat, I hate it. I feel simultaneously bored and anxious.

Sage: Yes. Remember, the ego-I always opposes what IS.

Not-enough-time equals
urgency and stress.

Too-much-time equals
boredom.

All-the-time-result equals
suffering!

MASSIVE RESISTANCE

comes up against meditation, silence, solitude and anything else that allows for gaps in doing. A person controlled by egocentric karmic conditioning/self-hate must, above all else, be kept busy, preferably urgently busy.

Conditioned mind needs a constant doer with something to constantly do in order to constantly avoid the present.

Student: I see why meditation is so important. In that silence there is nothing to do and ego-I goes crazy. We can watch it happen and see it for what it is.

Sage: Yes!

Resistance to Practicing When Things Are Going Well

Student: I came to practice when I was really suffering. And now things are going pretty well. I don't hear voices yelling at me. My life is way better. I'm enjoying myself. I feel a lot of resistance to keeping up my practice commitments when it feels like there's no reason to. Do I have to practice all the time? Couldn't I just take a break once in a while?

Sage: A geographical metaphor might be useful here. Picture a meandering river.

As the river meanders across the valley, it deposits the sand and silt from the riverbeds on the narrow neck where the river bends. The curve of the river gets gradually separated from the main course of the river and a small lake is formed, isolated from the river's course, cut off from the source of water.

Life is the river. It never stops flowing. The silt deposits are our karmic tendencies.

When we begin practice ego has cut us off from the flow of Life. We haven't been paying attention, we've been unconscious, the grooves of karmic conditioning have been reinforced, and the separation has formed. Practice allows us to keep the channels to the source open. When we stop practicing, the silt of karmically conditioned ignorance builds again. We go unconscious, and when we wake up one day we realize all our hard-earned clarity and awareness are no longer available and we must start over.

The voices are rooting for us to go unconscious, talking us into "taking a break." That's how karma will continue to be created and maintained.

Student: So I guess I don't get to take a break.

Sage: **Only something that is not supportive of you would want you to take a break from what takes care of you.** The ego-identity maintenance system wins when you "quit while ahead." The human gets left behind to suffer.

Student: So the way it gets me is to convince me I need to pay attention only when there's something specific I have to accomplish. When that's over, I shouldn't have to make any effort.

Sage: Yes. The ego-identity maintenance system operates incessantly--that's one of its primary characteristics. If you were always paying attention to **thisherenow**, ego would be out of business. Given that, it wants your attention on a conversation about effort and quitting and breaks so you will go unconscious as it continues to build the karmic silt deposits that cut you off from the river of Life.

> **Being present in Life is effortless,**
> **and it's the only thing in life that is!**

So, permission to go unconscious is denied.

Resistance and the Illusion of Control

Student: I feel frustrated that I can't make this meditation stuff work.

Sage: I know it's difficult to accept that we can't control circumstances any more than we can control ourselves! To get past resistance we have to relinquish the myth of control.

Control is defined as
the power to influence or direct behavior
or the course of events.
The fact is there is no such power.

Privileged conditioned human beings are deeply programmed to believe that control is possible. It's difficult for us to accept that control is only an idea, an illusion. We're conditioned to believe we have agency and that we can and should change what is.

Much of the time, for many of us, our experience seems to support the idea that we have control. I want to get something from the grocery store, I drive there, the store has what I want, I buy it, and I drive home. Of course I'm in control of my Life. It can **appear** as if we have control right up to the time it becomes obvious we don't. The car won't start, I have a flat tire, I'm in an accident...

It is compassionate to all
to face the fact
that "having control of Life"
is a myth of ego.

Student: Wow, I never thought of that. I've never considered "things going wrong" as proof of lack of control larger than "I made a mistake, I should have done something different, I should have known better." I've always believed things didn't go the way they should because I did something wrong.

Sage: Well, that is the point of the process of "something wrong, feeling bad." That process keeps us from seeing what's actually happening.

Student: Which is...?

Sage: When we are present, squarely in the middle of the moment as it arises, it's obvious we have no control over how that's happening. And, it's clear that the idea that anything else is possible is an illusion.

Student: So I hear you saying that when we're caught in the illusion of an alternate reality, we believe that "I" can actually change it.

ALTERNATE REALITY

Sage: And, if we **can't** manifest or materialize what we want, there's something wrong. Stuck in this process, we are unable to see the futility of that position, and we fail to realize nothing in Life can be different from the way it is.

Having said that, control **is happening in our lives.**

RESISTANCE

Caught in egocentric karmic conditioning, **we are being controlled,** and what is controlling our life experience is ego. As long as we believe ego-identity is who we are, we are in resistance to Life as Life is, suffering as a consequence of not being able to control something that cannot be controlled.

The trap this orientation keeps us in is the illusion that one process leads to another. If I work hard, I'll have money. If I learn to meditate, I'll have peace. If I'm a good person, I'll get what I want. In that trap we don't see that the conditional relationships between two things only **seem** to be true in an imaginary world ego creates. Nothing in Life is conditionally related. Everything simply is.

We will never have the life we want through doing something that will get us the life we want.

The secret
to having the life we want
is to have the life we want.

Student: So all we have is the life we have. And my best way to get past resistance is to drop the myth that I have control and drop the conversation that is controlling me!

Sage: Yes. Trying to control Life, manipulate it, and make it what we want it to be guarantees that we will never have the Life we want.

AWARENESS
The Antidote to Resistance

Student: I've been looking at resistance in many different ways, and it's been really helpful. But I'm not sure it has led to being any happier.

Sage: Hmmm... Let me tell you a story...

There once was a seeker who decided to go to a monastery. The teacher assigned her to work in the garden. Her job was to tend it and make sure it was weeded.

The student began, eager to be of service.

After a couple of months, one of the other monks pointed out to the student that the monastery no longer had flowers for the altar or vegetables for the table. "Do you not know the difference between a flower or vegetable and a weed?" the monk asked.

The student stood in stunned silence for a moment. She returned to the teacher and asked, "How do I know which one is a weed?"

She was given the teaching that enabled her to discern a weed from a flower or a vegetable.

Several years went by and the garden was yielding beautiful flowers and delicious vegetables. People far and wide knew of the achievements of the talented gardener.

Eventually, the seeker returned again to the teacher saying, "I am weary. Please give me another task. The garden is so full of weeds! Though I spend all my time weeding, I cannot keep up. I am tired and angry and so frustrated!"

The teacher replied, "Go back to the garden; love the flowers and honor the vegetables."

Several months later, the teacher was walking past the garden and saw the student. She laughed, she hummed, she sang. The song was one of wonder at the beauty of the flowers and the ripeness of the tomato.

The teacher stopped and asked the student, "What about the weeds?"

The student pointed to a pile of weeds and said smiling, "I just pick them up and lay them aside and let them know it is time for them to go."

When we come to practice we have to learn how we cause ourselves to suffer. It is important for us to understand what we are up against, to see the process by which the illusion of a separate self is created and maintained, and to see how resistance keeps the ego-identity (the weeds) alive.

The ego-identity maintenance system is programmed to keep us in its clutches. The danger is that if we don't pay close attention we can end up feeding the karma and keeping it alive, while believing we are working out our salvation.

If we're not careful,
we will miss the beauty
of the garden
because we're focused
on the weeds.

Our practice can be one of these three.

1. Being a weed
and obsessing about weeding

Practice can be focused on egocentric karmic conditioning/self-hate and our relationship with it ⇒

what it does, how it does it,
what it says, how it says it,
what we feel when it says what it says,
how it changes the way it does what it does.

We blame ego-I for our behaviors and believe we are doing Awareness Practice.

But that is the practice of being in the "process of suffering," not in the "process of ending suffering." Recognizing weeds is an important step, but we don't want our attention to be limited to weeds.

We could call this stage
"conditioning monitoring conditioning,"

2. Being in the garden and working with weeds

This, too, is an important phase of practice, the phase in which we practice **disidentification**. Here we become more deeply aware of ⇒

what the voices say,
how conditioning works,
and how our karma plays out.

We realize that our true nature is not conditioning or karma. We see that what we are is that which notices.

Disidentification is such a powerful place in practice because it is possible to see, hear, and feel all the human being is suffering without being identified with the suffering or with the person who suffers. It is important to realize that this is a phase from which we can move on.

We could call this phase
"awareness observing conditioning."

3. Being in the garden and being in love with the garden.

We train the attention to be with awareness. The practice is not just being aware that we are that which notices, it is living that awareness and experiencing Life as that which animates all. We never leave the beauty of the garden, no matter what shows up in it.

We could call this phase
"awareness attending to awareness."

The way out of suffering
is to be engaged in
the process of
ending suffering.

In other words, we move to living in love of the flowers and in the wonder of the bees, and in the song of the wind and the dance of the butterfly.

To pluck the weed and lay it aside, we don't have to leave awareness of the beauty of the garden or our love of the flowers. When we encounter the weed, we recognize it for what it is, accept it, lay it aside, and let it go.

It is not true that transcendence is possible only through resistance, through overcoming something. The illusion that Life is not living us, that we are not the Intelligence that animates, and that we are separate from Life is the illusion we are transcending--no resistance required!

However, it does take PRACTICE.

What follows is a series of practices that will assist us to train the attention on awareness, drop resistance to the weeds, and live in acceptance of all of Life.

As we practice with these exercises, we might keep in our awareness another principle we have explored previously:

the process
IS
the outcome.

In Life, the transformation occurs in the **process**. This is, no doubt, why the ego-identity maintenance strategy is so focused on preventing us from ever getting started or keeping to a program of any kind.

Suggestion: Copy this page
and hang it where you will see it often.

TOOLS
FOR GARDEN LIVING

A 30-Day Retreat

15 exercises, each done for 2 days

1. Feeding the Good Wolf

An old Cherokee is teaching her grandson about Life. "A fight is going on inside me," she said to the boy. "It is a terrible fight between two wolves. One is evil. It is anger, envy, sorrow, regret, greed, arrogance, self-pity, guilt, resentment, inferiority, lies, false pride, superiority, shame, and fear.

The other is good. It is joy, peace, love, hope, serenity, humility, kindness, benevolence, empathy, generosity, gratitude, compassion, and trust. The same fight is going on inside you and inside every other person."

The grandson thought about it for a minute and asked, "Which wolf will win?"

The old Cherokee smiled and quietly said, "The one you feed."

We have seen that resistance is simply a way to ensure that the ego-I and its illusory existence are maintained. We experience resistance when we set out to do something that will take care of us, such as meditation, healthy eating, exercise, and Awareness Practice. When we believe what the voices of egocentric karmic conditioning/self-hate tell us and act accordingly, we feed the karmic system. We reinforce its grooves and increase the probability that we will continue to act from that place of conditioning.

Almost every strategy ego-I uses to maintain itself is in the service of hijacking the attention. When the attention is on the conditioned story, we are lost in the world of ego. Like a muscle that is being trained, we have to practice training the attention to live in awareness; we have to practice building new pathways so that attention will default to Life instead of traipsing the old, tired grooves of karma. We have to practice deepening our ability to have the experience we choose to have.

Assignment: Feed the good wolf.

In Awareness Practice we are learning to direct our attention to choosing and feeding the good wolf. Remember: what we feed (attend to) is what we have.

 You may wish to record and listen to this as a guided imagery.

Find a quiet place, sit down, take several long deep breaths, and begin to get in touch with your good wolf. See yourself in moments of kindness, generosity, gratitude, and happiness. Feel what it feels like to love and empathize, to be patient and caring. As you become aware of those feelings, spend a few moments breathing that good feeling into and around your body.

Now, spend the next 48 hours feeding the good wolf.
-- Stop listening to the voices of what's not working, something wrong, and not enough.
-- Focus attention on what's "right" and what's working, that unseen world of constant support that includes all those "good wolf feelings."

-- Make a note of all that "yes, it's working" support: the car that starts, the food that's there when you're hungry, the water that comes out of the tap, shelter from the elements, kind words, smiles from a stranger, assistance in accomplishing tasks.

Record and Listen to how you feel when the attention is on the process of feeding the good wolf. See how you are supported in doing what you set out to do, and how little room there is for resistance when you're with the good wolf.

2. Loving what you seek

A spiritual teacher once said to her two pupils, "What you are seeking is represented as an iron needle buried in a haystack. You must find the needle. Think it over and let me know how you would go about looking for it."

When they came back the next day, the first student said he would set fire to the haystack and wait for the wind to blow the ashes away. "Your path is the path of the recluse," responded the master. "It is a true path if heroically pursued to the end, but it does seem to be a waste of hay!"

The second student explained her approach. She would take straws from the stack one by one, inspect them and feel them until she found the iron needle. "The path of philosophical analysis," said the teacher, "also a true one that requires immense patience, detachment and continuous awareness."

"Is there another way?" asked the students.

"Yes," the teacher replied. "If you carry a magnet around the haystack, pausing frequently, you will feel a tiny quiver in the magnet you hold. There is a quiver in the iron also, but you do not yet know about that. If you follow the tiny quiver of your magnet, it will become stronger, and you will be drawn directly to where the needle is hidden. The magnet you hold and the needle you  are seeking will leap joyously to become one and your search will be rewarded."
-- Adapted from *Encounters with Yoga and Zen*

Resistance rears its ugly head the moment we decide to do something that lights us up. We are given a laundry list of all the reasons that we should not embark on what we set out to do. Finally, we give up because the voices convince us that it's too hard and it would take too much time, be too much work. We abandon our lives and ourselves when we resist what lights us up.

Through the lens of conditioned mind we cannot see that Life is a force of attraction, love, and resonance.　Instead of resisting what causes us to suffer, Life invites us to practice being in love with what we seek.

Life is not hard, it simply is.　Being present to it is our natural state, and from that place we can, in the words of Joseph Campbell, "follow our bliss."

Life attracts Life, and we quiver in response to Life's force flowing through our human form.　We can practice recognizing and cultivating that quiver because that is what we are.

Assignment: Magnetic resonance

-- How does your magnetic attraction to Life manifest?

-- When do you feel resonance?　What in Life causes you to quiver in response?

-- Practice looking for what you are drawn to and cultivate an orientation to Life that is attraction instead of resistance.

How does this practice assist you in working with a "problem" in which "I don't want to and I don't feel like it," has been your primary response?

3. The universe is friendly.

The Buddha taught that the root cause of suffering is avidya, ignorance of our true nature. We perceive ourselves falsely as a "someone," a self separate from all that is, and our suffering stems from this loss of knowledge of our authenticity.

This illusion of a separate self, the "I," is a survivor in a hostile world filled with scarcity, deprivation, strife, fear and self-hate. Our conditioned experience is one of deep hunger, alienation, isolation and loneliness. We set out to acquire, defeat, relate, achieve, and work as means to satisfy a deep longing that is central to an illusion of separation.

We live in exile, unaware of our "place in the family of things," haunted by a feeling of not belonging. When we are identified with the separate self, we feel separation from Life. We are needy, we want, we desire. Everyone we interact with is someone from whom we want something--anything to fill that deep hunger.

When we step out of that world and into Life, there's nothing to want any longer. Because we are in Life, we are fulfilled. Life is living us. There is no separation. We cease to want and need things from other people. We seek to be with a community, in relationship, not because we **want** to belong, but because we **do** belong. Relating and participating mirrors where we want to live--here, present in Life, practicing wanting only what is.

When we stop identifying with the conditioned aspects of ourselves, when we stop believing the voices of self-hate, what's left is a deep sense of belonging.

Assignment: Friendly universe
Albert Einstein is supposed to have said that the most important question we can ask is whether the universe is friendly.

You may wish to record and listen to this imagery.

Find a quiet place and make yourself comfortable. Close your eyes. Take a couple of nice, long, deep breaths and allow to arise in awareness a time in your life when you experienced the world as friendly, when you were aware of its abundance, when you felt its kindness and received its compassion. Recall a time when you felt resonance, beauty, and harmony, at peace with all that is. Breathe in the experience of belonging to Life, of being animated by Intelligence, of simply being present to what arises in each moment.

For the next two days, live as if the universe is friendly. What does that feel like? How does that orientation change how you might look at something that you were resisting?

4. Living Life's guidance

We are trained to consult egocentric karmic conditioning/self-hate as the expert on the reality we inhabit. We seldom question what it's telling us. We feel tremendous resistance to change, to trying something outside our comfort zone, to experimenting with something different or learning something new. The conversation in our heads talks us out of a direct experience of Life.

Being present allows us to be open to Life's Intelligence. We've all experienced the mysterious process of questions being magically answered, problems being solved, and insights about thorny issues dropping quietly into awareness. When we are not tuned in to the ego-identity maintenance system, there is a wealth of information, practical, useful, and mystical that Life is constantly making available.

When we tune in to Life's wisdom we feel alive. Each moment is fresh and new and filled with possibility. There is always something interesting to learn and we are in love with simply finding out. This curiosity, this thrill of adventure, this spirit of inquiry, this joy of discovery is an orientation that we left behind in childhood.

Assignment: Not knowing

Reclaiming our sense of "not knowing" is a way to be in Life, to live in insight, to experience being lived by the Intelligence that animates all. It is trusting Life to tell us what we need to know.

For the next 48 hours, get in touch with all you do not know. Be curious. Ask questions. Notice how much of what you say and do comes from unexamined beliefs and assumptions that keep the illusory world of karmic conditioning alive.
-- Are you listening to karmic conditioning?
-- Can you tune in to Life's teachings and have a direct experience of living in guidance with Life as your teacher?

How does this attitude liberate you from the tyranny of a problem that you could not solve and have given up on because ego-identity has talked you into "I don't want to, I don't feel like it"?

5. Living in Gasshō

In the Zen tradition, we bring our hands together at the heart and bow. This is called Gasshō. Each hand symbolizes a heart. In bringing the hands together we are saying "your heart and my heart are one." In bowing we acknowledge the oneness of all things, that everything is the Buddha, and that we are all simply unique expressions of the same Intelligence.

Our experience of Life is usually quite different from "living in gasshō" because most of us are conditioned to view Life through the lens of ego. "I am" separates me from all that is and from everyone else. That separation colors the way we view the world, which is as separate things. We are conditioned to look at how things are different, not how things are similar.

To maintain the illusion of separation, the ego-identity incessantly scans for differences. It is a process of constant comparison. I don't write as well as she does; I'm better than he is at controlling emotions, and so forth. Comparing is rooted in a belief in scarcity and sets up a context of competing for survival--if we are inherently different, then we must maintain the differences. One point of view (represented by "me" as ego-identity) against another point of view (represented by "you" as ego-identity) is what it comes down to; there is no room in this illusory world for both points of view. "I" can only survive at "your" expense. That mutually exclusive orientation serves only to maintain the illusion of separation.

 A meditation teacher was invited to speak at a small gathering. She told the assembled students that they must strive to acquire freedom from strong reactions to the events of daily life, an attitude of habitual reverence, and a regular meditation practice, all of which she explained in detail. "The object," she said, "is to realize the one divine Life manifesting as all things, not only in the meditation period, but also in daily life. The whole process is like filling a sieve with water."

The group had many reactions to this instruction, ranging from being bemused to feeling criticized to being cynically dismissive of the teaching. Only one student decided to ask the teacher for clarification.

The teacher took the student to the seashore and gave him a cup and a sieve.

"Show me how you fill it with water," she instructed the student.

The student bent down and scooped water into the sieve with the cup. The water, of course, immediately drained through the sieve.

The teacher said, "It's just like that with spiritual practice. We stand on the rock of I-ness and try to ladle divine realization into it. This is not the way to fill the sieve with water or the self with the divine Life."

"How do you do it then?" asked the student

The teacher flung the sieve far out into the sea where it quickly sank.

"Now it's full of water," she said, "and it will remain so. That's the way to fill it with water, and it's the way to do spiritual practice. It's not ladling little cupfuls of divine Life into individuality, but throwing individuality far out into the divine sea of Life."
-- Adapted from *Encounters with Yoga and Zen*

Assignment: Live in Gasshō
As a process, resistance separates. It is essentially a process of assessment, evaluation, judgment and criticism. It looks for differences.

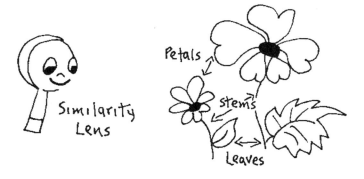

Similarity Lens

Petals

stems

Leaves

For the next 48 hours, choose reminders for yourself: a color, a sound such as the phone ringing, a familiar behavior such as opening a door. As you go about your day, when you are present to the reminder, consciously switch from looking for differences to acknowledging the similarities between things. (Flowers, trees, animals, people--all breathe, all seek that which supports Life. Light and sound are energy vibrations.)

-- Bow in gasshō (literally or metaphorically) as you acknowledge the oneness of all things.
-- Honor the sacredness of all things.
-- Practice reverence.

Watch how resistance melts away as you practice realizing the oneness of all Life.

6. Empty Tea Cup

An earnest young student travels to a distant land to learn from a wise Zen teacher.

He arrives at the Monastery, eager to begin his training, impatient to get his questions answered. In his first audience, he peppers the teacher with dozens of questions. The teacher remains silent. Every subsequent meeting with the teacher happens the same way. The student gets increasingly frustrated and angry. He finally storms into the teacher's room and demands an explanation.

The teacher hands the student a teacup and then begins to pour the tea. He does not stop. The teacup overflows.

 When the student cries out in horror, the teacher says, "You are like this cup, too full. Unless you are empty, how can you receive anything from me?"
-- Old Zen Story

"I" is a closed position, an over-flowing teacup that prevents us from being open to Life as it is. The Buddha taught that clinging to this point of view, defending it as the only point of view, causes us to suffer.

Assignment: Empty your teacup

My Point of View

For the next 48 hours practice dropping a point of view that constitutes your cup of "I." (Examples: Life is hard, people are selfish, I'll never have what I want, I've got to look out for # 1, etc.) Step out of it and see if you can view Life from a different perspective. What possibilities arise when Life is not viewed from the narrow limits of egocentric karmic conditioning/self-hate?

Experience the freedom that comes from not having to defend a point of view or resist someone else's point of view.

7. Living in Abundance

We often define egocentric karmic conditioning/self-hate as "something, wrong, not enough." If we listen long enough to the voices, we come to believe that the world we live in is one of deprivation and scarcity. We desire something different, we want to change our circumstances and ourselves, and we are convinced that doing what the voices tell us to do will make that possible.

Zen writer Alan Watts defines "want" as lack. "Wanting" something points to the lack of it. When identified with conditioning, we are in a state of desire, a state of want, a state of lack.

For example, if I am a perfectionist my desire for perfection (through the lens of the ego-identity maintenance system) is always causing me to focus on what is not perfect. I am always experiencing the absence of perfection. I completely miss the perfection of Life as it is unfolding in each moment.

Photography is a useful metaphor, though not so much in the digital age! Everyone is familiar with the negative. It is the stencil, if you will, capturing the absence of light. Viewing  Life through the dark "negative" of egocentric karmic conditioning/self-hate keeps us trapped in seeing only scarcity and absence, instead of the glorious generosity and abundance of Life.

Each of us is summoned forth from our "wrappings" to be a unique expression of Life, a perfect part of a glorious whole. The world offers itself joyously, repeatedly extending an invitation to revel in abundance. In opening to Life, in receiving its gifts, we experience ourselves as whole and holy, a sacred part of all that is.

Assignment: Live in abundance

Find a quiet comfortable place. Close your eyes and open to Life's abundance. Drink from the deep cup of Life's generosity.

-- What is Life giving you?
-- How has Life supported you?
-- Make a list of what you are grateful for.

For the next 48 hours, practice being open to receiving Life's generosity. Can resistance be maintained in the face of gratitude?

8. Being

Being is an unfamiliar state. Most conditioned humans feel acute discomfort when faced with "nothing to do." We idealize that state but seldom enjoy it. In fact, a morning of sitting on the beach watching the waves can be a guilty pleasure that we feel we have to apologize for.

Doing in the conditioned world translates into worthiness, purpose, accomplishment, a validation of existence, of being somebody. It is the busy people who are valued. "I" feel important if "I" have insufficient time, an incomplete project list, a mountain of unanswered emails, and my nose in my cell phone answering texts and juggling calls.

Feeling rested, relaxed and refreshed, and without an inclination to action is to be viewed with trepidation, a sign that one is degenerating into a lazy-good-for-nothing. The voices justify their existence by telling us that were it not for them, we would all give into the siren song and be forever lost in the land of the Lotus-eaters.

Absence of doing allows space for the movement of Life, to tune in to the rhythm beyond tick-tock.

Being is spacious, timeless; it's relaxed grace, effortless unfolding, a perfect symphony of movement and stillness. Only that which attempts to be outside of Life needs to create rigid structures, permanence (there is no such thing), and timelines to gloss over the abyss of the moments between existences. Being is the awareness of effortless movement. This practice is one of being.

Assignment: Just being.
For the next 48 hours, notice how conditioned impulses are focused on "doing," and set the intention to drop the impulse to do. Sit down and experience "being" for a minute, 5 minutes, an hour. Please do not meditate--that is also doing!

Enjoy the movement of the present moment. How does "just being" change the orientation of having to do something about a "problem" that you don't feel like addressing?

9. For the sheer joy of it

We often feel tremendous resistance to doing something "just because." In the world of egocentric karmic conditioning/self-hate there must be a reason, a meaning, a purpose, or an outcome for anything we do. The voices focus us on results. And when the results don't materialize, it is an opportunity for self-hate to beat us up and tell us it's our fault. In fact, if we embark on something and don't make progress towards a goal (set up by conditioning) then we are told that the effort is not worthwhile. Doing something just for the love or joy of doing it is seen as a waste of time. We are promised the joy when we get the results and are seldom allowed simply to enjoy the process.

The voices do not encourage delight. When we are present and participating in Life for the sheer joy of being alive, there is no place for the ego-I to exist. When we practice being wholeheartedly present in thisherenow, we are not practicing ego-identity maintenance.

The breath is a powerful example in Awareness Practice for just this reason. We breathe in, we breathe out. It doesn't lead to anything. We're not going to get to some place where we can stop needing to breathe all the time.

Assignment: Being delighted.
For 48 hours, practice being delighted. Do whatever you are engaged in for the joy of it, and do it wholeheartedly. Experience the wonder of being alive, of being breathed by Life.

Notice the absence of resistance in wholehearted delight.

10. Offering

"All of us are unique expressions of Life's Intelligence."

Do you feel resistance to that statement? Conditioning wants to dismiss a statement like that because our self-image, our identity, is not that we are unique in a let's-celebrate-that sense. It's more there's-something-wrong-with-you-that-needs-to-be-fixed.

Conditioning constantly compares us to other people, judging us as deficient in some way or highlighting differences favorable to us and then making us feel bad for thinking we're superior. If we are complimented for something we did well, it wants us to be self-effacing and humble and deflect (and therefore not take in) the approbation. If someone criticizes us, even for the very same "deficiencies" conditioning criticizes us for, we are meant to be defensive.

Comparison serves to keep the ego-identity in place. In the words of Bhagwan Shree Rajneesh: "The ego cannot exist without comparison, hence if you really want to drop the ego, drop comparing. You will be surprised; where has the ego gone? Compare, and it is there; and it is there only in comparison. It is not an actuality; it is a fiction created out of comparison."

Denying our authenticity is a fundamental form of resistance. It maintains the illusion of separation. We experience ourselves as unworthy of receiving anything and far too inadequate to **offer** anything. We are not allowed to be the unique expression of Life that we are, which is what we are here to **offer**.

Offering ourselves as brilliant and unique expressions of Life, not less or more than all other Life expressions, affirms the truth of the brilliance of all things. In oneness, only brilliance exists. There is no concept of "more or less brilliant." There is no division, no comparison, no possibility of judgment.

Assignment: Offer yourself to Life

Experience yourself as all that you are, a beautiful expression of the Intelligence that animates, a perfect offering.

-- Make a list of what Life has given you to bring to life.

-- How will you practice offering what you are?

Hello Life!

I am available!

As you do this practice, look to see how accepting yourself as an authentic expression of Life creates willingness to support yourself in doing what you set out to do. Notice how different this is from the resistance of "I don't want to, I don't feel like it."

11. Taking care of the self

Selfishness is universally condemned. If we look closely at some of the things dismissed as "selfish" by the voices of egocentric karmic conditioning/self-hate, we see how cleverly the ego-identity is maintained at the expense of the authentic being.

For example, I am exhausted and I can't summon the energy to visit my sick mother. It's likely the voice in my head is going to beat me up if I choose to postpone the visit and take care of myself first. Or I decide to get a massage and feel guilty for taking time off while my hardworking business partner is burning the midnight oil. If I don't choose my responsibilities to family, work, social circle, religious institution or pets above taking care of myself, I am just the wrong person. Health, fitness, nutrition, spiritual practice and well-being are all sacrificed at the altar of ego.

Condemning "selfishness" is ego-identity's way of excluding the authentic human from genuine care. Of course, the ego-identity maintenance system is a master of faux caregiving. It talks us into junk food, eating sweets, missing our exercise routine, or vegetating in front of the tv screen under the guise of "taking care of myself" and "giving myself a break." It's all an elaborate way of preserving its existence, while ensuring our needs are never met.

The way we use the word compassion in this practice is "to suffer with." It is not sympathy or pity. It is admiration and appreciation for the courage to face what IS without a desire to have anything be different. It is the ultimate projection of adequacy, and it is possible only when we come from authenticity, wholeness and non-separation.

We cannot truly "be compassion" if we exclude ourselves from the equation.

Excluding this authentic being only serves to maintain the illusion of an "I" that is separate from everything else, and it effectively prevents the inclusion of anyone else.

We can offer compassion only when we are able to include ourselves in unconditional love and acceptance.

Assignment: Take care of the authentic being.

Find a quiet, comfortable place and close your eyes. Take a couple of nice, long, deep breaths. Feel your shoulders relax. Feel yourself animated by Life's compassion.

For the next couple of days, practice prioritizing the authentic being.
-- Do what takes care of you.
-- Allow yourself to feel given to by Life.
-- Be kind to yourself.
-- Practice unconditional love and acceptance for the human form.

Feel the joy of affirming your authenticity instead of denying and resisting it.

12. Acceptance

In Awareness Practice, we are encouraged to develop the ability to direct the attention. When attention is here, in the moment, instead of on the conversation in conditioned mind, we are fully present to Life as it is. In other words we are accepting what Life is instead of resisting it.

Life says, This way! →

Ego-I says, ← That way!

Resistance is the maintenance of an illusion of Life as it **should** be. Acceptance of Life as IS, is the antithesis of resistance. Authentic being is unconditional love and acceptance.

Ego-I at this point will rush in with arguments against accepting the "unacceptable." As we said earlier, we are talking about the **process of acceptance** not the limited notion of acceptable and unacceptable into which conditioned mind divides the world.

Ego-I would say that if we accept everything we have

to say yes to everything. But compassionate
acceptance implies an appropriate Life response.

When Life says "no," saying no is saying yes.

Here's an example. I don't want to continue in my
relationship because it no longer takes care of
either of us. If I am listening to the voices, I might
hear that I should stay in it because I made a
commitment. That is translated as I must stay with
it, no matter how bad it is or how unhappy we are.
If I'm listening to Life, the appropriate response to
accepting the state of my relationship could very
well be to leave it.

Just being present to what IS is a relaxing way to
be lived. Life ceases to be a struggle for control
over circumstances. We realize how much energy,
effort, focus and attention it takes to maintain
suffering. The voices would argue that it takes
great effort to be with conscious compassionate
awareness. But the fact is it takes far more
energy to maintain the voices--we are just used to
making the effort. That effort drains and

depresses us, leaving us worn out and tired at the end of the day.

Just
sit there right now.
Don't do a thing. Just rest.

For your separation from God
is the hardest work in this world.
  ---Hafiz

It takes far less energy (none actually) to be with Life as it lives us. That's why centered people are so energetic and lit up!

Assignment: Have an acceptance energy drink
For the next 48 hours, practice acceptance. What does it feel like to be present to what is unfolding without feeling the need to control, alter or fix it in any way?

Do you notice how much less effort there is in simply relaxing into Life than being in resistance to it?

13. Play

"Man suffers only because he takes seriously what the gods make fun off."
-- Alan Watts.

"God is a comedian playing to an audience afraid to laugh."
-- Voltaire

In the ancient texts, it is said that the reality we project, the illusion of separation we live in and wake up from, is created in the spirit of play. Our part is to gloriously play the role we are given and never lose sight of the fact that we are "mere actors." Ego-I takes itself and its survival very seriously and strips the fun out of living.

Assignment: Life's play

Get out a notebook or journal. Find a quiet place and answer these questions.

--What is the title of your personal drama?

--Who are the players?

--What are the roles?

--How does ego-identity script the parts and direct the action?

For the next 48 hours, joyfully embrace the spirit of play. How much fun can you have with whatever you are doing when you are **not** acting out the script of ego-I but wholeheartedly participating in the play of Life?

What happens to resistance when we approach life as a play?

14. Project adequacy

The Buddha taught that we are here to work out our own salvation diligently. Implicit in that teaching is that we are fully equipped to do so, that we are adequate to our Life experience. In fact, throughout our Life path, we are encountering exactly what we need to transcend, should we choose to.

ADEQUATE
HUMAN
BEING

On the other hand, ego-I presents itself as supremely inadequate. It is focused on altering life circumstances in order to avoid what Life is presenting.

The greatest gift that we can experience is to be in the presence of someone who mirrors our adequacy and models "there is nothing wrong," no matter how intense, painful, or violent our emotions. When we are mirrored in that way, we are given permission to experience our adequacy, to find our ability to accept any sensation arising in Life and simply be present to it.

Assignment: Be adequate

For the next 48 hours, step into the adequacy of your authentic being. Practice being present to life circumstances as they are instead of resisting, denying, avoiding or attempting to change them.

From that place of adequacy, see if you can model "there is nothing wrong" for someone. Experience how relaxing it is simply to "be there" for someone instead of inhabiting a conditioned attitude of "needing to take care of them" in any way.

15. The Attitude of Practice

"If something is worth doing, it's
worth doing with two hands."
-- Zen saying

This teaching is pointing to the benefits of being fully
present and committed to whatever we are engaged
with. There is intense resistance to the idea of
committing to something that requires sustained
effort. Instant gratification is a staple in the world
of ego. Fast foods, cliff notes, the 15-second
commercial, and multi-tasking, are examples of a
conditioned approach of skimming over Life instead
of participating in each moment wholeheartedly.

It takes years to perfect a craft. A craftsperson
focuses on creating beauty and understands the
patience and wholeheartedness required to create a
masterpiece.

Our lives are masterpieces. We get talked out of
wholeheartedly appreciating and participating in the
unfolding of that perfection.

Assignment: An attitude of wholeheartedness

For the next 48 hours, see if you can do whatever you are doing with two hands. What does it feel like to commit to something wholeheartedly?

Notice how being completely present and attentive leaves no room for the voices of resistance.

Life's Masterpiece

Bonus Round

Here are a few more assignments that will enable you to continue the retreat for another week.

16. Don't feel bad.

When we are identified with egocentric karmic conditioning/self-hate, any input is taken personally. The ego-identity maintenance system scrambles the information and makes it mean something about "me," usually something bad.

Assignment: Feel good.
Spend 24 hours practicing no self-hate. Say no to feeling bad.

If there is no beating in the offing, if you cannot make a mistake, if there are no standards you have to meet, would you resist doing what your heart chooses?

17. Practice appreciation

The voices are harsh, critical, negative and judgmental. They are usually focused on what's wrong. Viewing the world through the lens of ego-I, we fail to see the beauty, simplicity, perfection, kindness, humor, innocence, and joy that is Life.

Assignment: Live in the appreciation corner

For the next 24 hours, practice bringing appreciation to the aspects of Life that egocentric karmic conditioning/self-hate has conditioned you to ignore, criticize, reject and find unacceptable.
-- Be ready to laugh.
-- Practice lovingkindness without exception.

Watch how resistance melts in the warm glow of appreciation.

APPRECIATION
CORNER

compassionate   kind
good   loving

CRITIC'S
CORNER

not good   lazy
enough
a failure
silly

18. Get over how you feel!

The world of ego-I is conditional. To be creative, I must feel inspired. Meditation is possible only when I feel calm and peaceful. I can relax only if I have finished my work. This resistance to action because a condition is not met is a clever ruse of the ego-I to ensure that we never write that poem, sit on the cushion, or relax. Through a constant conversation to focus the attention on the condition that needs to be met, the voices will keep us from ever finding out that the conditional relationship between two things is actually not true. We don't have to "do" something to be happy. The secret to being happy is to be happy.

Assignment: Get over how you feel!

For the next 48 hours practice getting over how you feel. Bust the myth that "we have to do x to feel y." -- See if you can have the experience you want to have by simply having the experience you want to have. If you are going on a walk to enjoy nature but feel irritable, turn your attention to enjoyment.

Does irritation, the "resistance to enjoyment," disappear?

⟹ Bonus points: Let yourself enjoy irritation!

19. Find the Middle Way

Conditioned mind always present us with extreme choices. By now, we can deduce why the ego-identity maintenance system presents choices this way! It's the perfect way to maximize resistance.

Here are some examples.

-- I have to go off sweets forever or give in to my sweet cravings forever and be overweight forever.

-- I have to stay in this job I hate or I'll be unemployed.

-- I have to make the best of this relationship or I am going to be alone for the rest of my Life!

> Focus on the extremes
> takes us away from the middle way
> that Life is offering in the moment.

So perhaps I cannot eat that fatty, sugary donut, but there are so many healthy sweets that I could learn to make and enjoy. Or perhaps I do eat that donut, and then I add extra exercise this week to burn off those calories. Or I try eating just one bite. (The last bite is the one we're left with, after all!) Lots of possibilities when we're present.

Assignment: Choose the Middle Way
For the next 48 hours, watch how the voices keep presenting extreme choices.

Instead of spending time in "I don't want to, I don't feel like it," see if you can stop and see a middle way, a choice that is compassionate for all.

20. Make a Life record

A good propaganda system
controls the story. We can
think of the ego-identity

maintenance system as the ultimate propaganda
machine. It works to be the narrative of record,
and all records kept are negative. Even a moment
of success is spun into a moment of failure. You
could have done better. You didn't deserve it. You
were lucky. It was only one time. What about all
those other failures?

Since we are conditioned to turn to ego-identity's
negative memory bank, we only get information
about what's wrong. There is resistance to anything
that is positive or Life-enabling because the
reference system itself is negative.

This is why we have to turn attention to something
else. Practice is not aimed at turning the negative
memory banks into positive memory banks. We
practice turning attention to the information source
that is Life.

Assignment: Set the record straight!

For the next 24 hours, stop listening to what the voices say and tune in to what Life has to say about your authentic being.

-- Celebrate your successes.

-- Make a Life Recording.

What does it feel like to be aligned with what is true, to be paddling with the current of the river of Life instead of paddling against it?

A REVIEW OF WHERE WE ARE

"What we call the beginning is often the end. And to make an end is to make a beginning. The end is where we start from."
-- T. S. Eliot

So let's review where we are...

There is an impulse to do something that would make a difference in the quality of our lives--a meditation practice, an exercise program, a better diet, less tv, no stress. Almost invariably we fall into a familiar loop: I don't want to. I don't feel like it. I can't. It's my fault. There is something wrong with me. I feel bad. I quit.

Encouraged to develop a practice of **noticing how this happens**, we see that what we want to do (lose weight, eat better, etc.) is irrelevant. There is an underlying, universal "**process of resistance.**"

Resistance is the experience of an ego-identity, an "I," a survival strategy, fighting to maintain itself. When we are **identified** with ego-I, we think it is who we are and our life experience is **ego-I's resistance to the threat of its extinction.**

Disidentification, stepping back and watching "how," gives us an experience other than ego-identity maintenance. We recognize the ways it manifests. We discover that the only outcome of identification is maintenance of suffering and dissatisfaction, keeping alive the illusion of separation and the imaginary possibility of a reality other than what IS.

If we do the exercises in the 30-day retreat in this book, we see there is a different way to be in life than we are conditioned to believe is possible. Instead of believing there is something wrong--with life, with "me," and with "my" circumstances--that has to be changed, fixed, or controlled to be ok, we find we can live in love, appreciation, delight, curiosity, compassion, adequacy, beauty, kindness, acceptance, belonging and joy.

These are the attributes of Life,
of the Intelligence that animates us,
of our authentic being.

It is possible to choose awareness
instead of resistance.
Switching attention
from the resistance
of ego-identity
to the Intelligence
that animates us
is a skill we can learn.

And it takes practice.

Paying attention is the practice of moving from being identified with ego-I to being in awareness.

Here is the recipe for making that movement:

Recipe for Practicing Awareness

Ingredients
- Attention
- Kindness
- Willingness
- Curiosity
- Commitment
- Joy

Directions

1 Be kind. 2. Learn to pay attention to what IS instead of the voice of what should be. 3. Commit to the practice. 4. Trust the process. 5. Be joyfully open and curious about what life is presenting in the moment.

An invitation from Life

When we are born we are issued an invitation: to recognize ourselves as a glorious expression of Life.

you are invited to Life.

We are free to decline or accept the invitation. If we accept the invitation, we are committing to a lifelong practice of **joyfully becoming what we are.**

Resistance will arise to making this choice, to this way of being, to practicing in each moment--the familiar "I don't want to, I don't feel like it." Ego-I will use any self-hating strategy (anxiety, fear, threats, rewards, distractions, fantasies, promises or beatings) to get us to resist Life's invitation.

But consider this for one moment:

What could be more important than accepting this invitation to be a glorious and unique expression of Life's Intelligence?

"You may believe you are out of harmony with Life and its eternal Now; but you cannot be, for you are Life and you exist Now--otherwise you would not be here. Hence the infinite Tao is something that you can neither escape by flight nor catch by pursuit; there is no coming toward it or going away from it; it is, and you are it. So, become what you are."
-- Alan Watts

So your final assignment, should you choose to accept it:

Say yes. Commit to a lifelong practice of becoming what you are--a joyful expression of Life's Intelligence. Fall in love with Life, accept Life's invitation, and experience the joy of Intelligence knowing itself.

THIS BOOK IN "OTHER WORDS."

Ego-Identity Is an Illusion.

Life is one, said the Buddha, and the Middle Way to the
end of suffering in all its forms is that which leads to
the end of the illusion of separation, which enables man
to see, as a fact as clear as sunlight, that all mankind,
and all other forms in manifestation, are one unit, the
infinitely variable appearance of an indivisible Whole.
-- Christmas Humphreys

There is only life. There is nobody who lives a life.
There is no such thing as a person. There are only
restrictions and limitations. The sum total of these
defines the person. You think you know yourself when
you know what you are. But you never know who you
are. The person merely appears to be, like the space
within the pot appears to have the shape and volume and
smell of the pot.
--Sri Nisargadatta Maharaj

What the caterpillar calls the end, the rest
of the world calls a butterfly.
-- Lao Tzu

Resistance Is Ego-Identity Maintenance

Acceptance is a synonym for being at one with what is.
Life is accepting. All life is clearly acceptable to Life.
Only human beings resist Life as it is.
-- Cheri Huber

The ego, our ordinary "initiator of action," is an
ephemeral construction, which in the unenlightened state
of awareness represents a kind of blockage or
impediment to the interplay of fundamental cosmic
forces. Because of our identification of ourselves with
the ego, what we ordinarily call action, or doing, cuts us
off from the complete reception of conscious energy in
our bodies and actions.
-- Jacob Needleman

People imagine that letting themselves go would have
disastrous results; trusting neither circumstances nor
themselves, which together make up life, they are forever
interfering and trying to make their own souls and the world
conform with preconceived patterns. This interference is
simply the attempt of the ego to dominate life. But when
you see that all such attempts are fruitless and when you
relax the fear-born resistance to life in yourself and around
you, which is called egoism, you realize the freedom of union
with Brahman.
--Alan Watts

Transcending Resistance

When I let go of what I am, I become what I might be.
-- Lao Tzu

To live in the Great Way is neither easy nor difficult,
but those with limited views are fearful and irresolute:
the faster they hurry, the slower they go, and clinging
cannot be limited: even to be attached to the idea of
enlightenment is to go astray. Just let things be in their
own way and there will be neither coming nor going.
Obey the nature of things (your own nature), and you
will walk freely and undisturbed.
-- Seng-ts'an

"Everything changes once we identify with being the
witness to the story, instead of the actor in it."
-- Ram Dass

The art of living...is neither careless drifting on the one
hand nor fearful clinging to the past on the other. It
consists in being sensitive to each moment, in regarding
it as utterly new and unique, in having the mind open and
wholly receptive.
-- Alan Watts

It takes Practice

Submit to a daily practice.
Your loyalty to that
is a ring on the door.

Keep knocking, and the joy inside
will eventually open a window
and look out to see who's there.
-- Rumi

We learn by practice. Whether it means to learn to
dance by practicing dancing or to learn to live by
practicing living, the principles are the same. One
becomes in some area an athlete of God.
-- Martha Graham

We come back to the moment over and over. That's
why we call this practice. We return again and again
until being here becomes not second nature, but what it
truly is, first nature.
-- Cheri Huber

Be patient with your practice. Trust in the Buddha way.
Throw yourself into your practice, yet with calmness and
composure. When conditions are right, when the fruit is
ripe, it naturally falls to the ground.
-- Jeff Shore

TALK WITH CHERI

Open Air
Talk Radio
Open Air is Cheri's internet-based call-in radio show.
Call in, listen, and download archived shows at
www.livingcompassion.org.

Online Classes
Cheri conducts interactive online classes via e-mail
on a wide variety of subjects
related to Zen Awareness Practice.
To be notified of future classes
sign up at www.livingcompassion.org.

Cheri's Practice Blog
Follow "Cheri Huber's Practice Blog"
at http://cherispracticeblog.blogspot.com

Books and Recordings
All Cheri Huber titles are available from your local
independent bookstore or online at sanghamarket.org/keepitsimple.
Also available online are audio recordings and DVDs.

What You Practice Is What You Have is a sequel to Cheri Huber's all-time bestseller, *There Is Nothing Wrong with You*, published in 1993. Over the years, many "There Is Nothing Wrong With You" retreats have been filled by those inspired by the book to look more deeply into how we can free ourselves from the ravages of conditioning and self-hate.

What You Practice Is What You Have further exposes the antics of conditioning and self-hate and introduces the Recording and Listening practice. Additional Awareness Practice tools, developed over the years by Cheri at the Zen Monastery Peace Center, are included.

What You Practice Is What You Have
ISBN 0-9710309-7-9

There Is Nothing Wrong With You
ISBN 0-9710309-0-1

There Is Nothing Wrong With You

An Extraordinary Eight-Day Retreat
based on the book
There Is Nothing Wrong With You: Going Beyond Self-Hate
by Cheri Huber

Inside each of us is a "persistent voice of discontent." It is constantly critical of life, the world, and almost everything we say and do. As children, in order to survive, we learned to listen to this voice and believe what it says.

This retreat, held at the beautiful Zen Monastery Peace Center near Murphys, California, in the western foothills of the Sierra Nevada, is eight days of looking directly at how we are rejected and punished by the voices of self-hate and discovering how to let that go. Through a variety of exercises and periods of group processing, participants gain a clearer perspective on how they live their lives and on how to find compassion for themselves and others.

This work is challenging, joyous, fulfilling, scary, courageous, demanding, freeing, loving, kind, and compassionate— compassionate toward yourself and everyone you will ever know.

For information on attending, contact:
Living Compassion/Zen Monastery Peace Center
P.O. Box 1756
Murphys, CA 95247
Ph.: 209-728-0860
Email: information@livingcompassion.org
Website: www.livingcompassion.org

ZEN MONASTERY PEACE CENTER

For a schedule of workshops and retreats and a list of our
meditation groups, contact us in one of the following ways.

Website: www.livingcompassion.org
Email: infomation@livingcompassion.org
Telephone: 209-728-0860

Zen Monastery Peace Center
P.O. Box 1756
Murphys, CA 95247

* * *

AFRICA VULNERABLE CHILDREN PROJECT

To find out about our work in an impoverished community
in Zambia, visit www.livingcompassion.org.

Visit www.livingcompassion.org to:

--Sign up to receive notice of new email classes with Cheri Huber

--See a schedule of workshops and retreats at the
Zen Monastery Peace Center in Murphys, CA.

--Read blogs with updates from
the Africa Vulnerable Children Project in Zambia

--Sign up for Reflective Listening Buddies

--Sign up for Practice Everywhere

--Participate in the Sangha Market

AND MUCH MORE

294.3444 Huber
Huber, Cheri
  I don't want to, I don't
feel like it
            30519009282503